Workbook

Joan Saslow ■ Allen Ascher

with Terra Brockman

PEARSON
Longman

Top Notch: English for Today's World   2
Workbook

Pearson Education, 10 Bank Street, White Plains, NY 10606

Editorial director: Pamela Fishman
Senior development editors: Trish Lattanzio, Martin Yu
Development editor: Geraldine Geniusas
Associate development editor: Siobhan Sullivan
Assisant development editor: Judy Li
Vice president, director of design and production: Rhea Banker
Director of electronic production: Aliza Greenblatt
Managing editor: Mike Kemper
Production editor: Michael Mone
Art director: Ann France
Senior manufacturing buyer: Dave Dickey
Photo research: Aerin Csigay
Text composition: Word & Image Design Studio, Inc.
Text font: 10/12 Frutiger
Cover photograph: "From Above," by Rhea Banker. Copyright © 2005 Rhea Banker.

ISBN: 0-13-110415-2

Photo Credits:

Page 1: (1) Will & Deni McIntyre/Getty Images, (2) Michael Goldman/Masterfile, (3) Robert Frerck/Odyssey Productions, Inc., (4) Jeff Greenberg/PhotoEdit; Page 4: Angelo Cavalli/Index Stock Imagery; Page 17: Reuters/Corbis; Page 20: Dan Gair/Index Stock Imagery; Page 25: (top) Kevin Fleming/Corbis, (middle) Wendell Metzen/Index Stock Imagery, (bottom) Royalty-Free/Corbis; Page 27: Fredde Lieberman; Page 30: Lawrence Manning/Corbis; Page 44: Steve Dunwell Photography, Inc./Index Stock Imagery; Page 47: The New Yorker Collection 1992 J.B. Handelsman from cartoonbank.com. All rights reserved; Page 53: Getty Images; Page 66: Index Stock Imagery; Page 68: (1) Heini Schneebeli/The Bridgeman Art Library International Ltd., (2) Stockbyte, (3) Dave G. Houser/Corbis, (4) The Art Archive/Dagli Orti(A)/Picture Desk, (5) The Art Archive/Egyptian Museum Turin/Jacqueline Hyde/Picture Desk, (6) Banco Mexicano de Imaagenes/The Bridgeman Art Library International Ltd., (7) David Young-Wolff/PhotoEdit, (8) Art Resource, NY; Page 70: Bettmann/Corbis; Page 72: (left to right) Heini Schneebeli/The Bridgeman Art Library International Ltd., The Art Archive/Dagli Orti(A)/Picture Desk, Tony Freeman/PhotoEdit, Banco Mexicano de Imaagenes/The Bridgeman Art Library International Ltd., Stockbyte, David Young-Wolff/PhotoEdit.

Illustration Credits:

Stephen Attoe: pages 5, 24, 39 (top), 50, 51, 64, 78, 86, 87 (top), 90, 22; Leanne Franson: pages 6, 32 (top), 43, 56, 87 (bottom); Brian Hughes: pages 29 (bottom), 31; Stephen Hutchings: pages 21, 57; Suzanne Mogensen: pages 23, 39 (bottom), 49; Dusan Petričic: pages 9, 27, 37, 88, 89; Steve Schulman: pages 68 (bottom), 84; Neil Stewart: pages 45, 75.

Printed in the United States of America
11 12 13 14 15–VHG–12 11 10 09 08

CONTENTS

Greetings and Small Talk

TOPIC PREVIEW

 Look at the pictures. Write the correct greeting under each picture. Use words from the box.

| bow | hug | kiss | shake hands |

1. _____ 2. _____ 3. _____ 4. _____

 Complete the conversation. Write the letter on the line.

A: You look familiar. Have we met before?

B: ____
    1.

A: Aren't you from Mexico?

B: ____
    2.

A: You know, I think we met at Joan's house last weekend.

B: ____
    3.

A: Yes, that's right. What have you been up to?

B: ____
    4.

a. Now I remember. You work with Joan.

b. As a matter of fact, I am.

c. Not too much.

d. I don't think so. I'm not from around here.

Read the conversation in Exercise 2 again. Circle the subjects they talk about.

family   religion   job   age   weather   nationality

 WHAT ABOUT YOU? **When you meet someone new, what subjects do you talk about? Put a ✔ next to the topics you usually talk about. Put an ✗ next to the topics you don't like to talk about.**

____ 1. my family   ____ 4. my age   ____ 7. politics

____ 2. my religion   ____ 5. my hometown or country   ____ 8. my job

____ 3. the weather   ____ 6. sports   ____ 9. other: _____

5 CHALLENGE. Write do's and don'ts for a visitor to your country about how to greet and address people, and what to talk about and what not to talk about.

LESSON 1

6 Complete each sentence with the present perfect. Use contractions when possible.

1. A: _____ any coffee
   you / have
   today?

   B: Yes, _____ two cups.
   I / have

2. A: _____ to any
   you / be
   foreign countries?

   B: Yes, _____ to Spain
   we / be
   and Morocco.

3. A: _____ this week?
   you / exercise

   B: Yes, _____ to the gym
   I / go
   twice.

4. A: _____ any good
   you / read
   books lately?

   B: No, _____ very busy.
   I / be

7 WHAT ABOUT YOU? Complete the questions with the correct form of the verbs from the box. Use each verb only once. Then write your <u>own</u> responses. When you answer <u>yes</u>, add specific information, using the simple past tense.

do	be	eat	meet	see

1. "Have you _____ any good movies lately?"
   (YOU) _____.

2. "Have you _____ any famous people?"
   (YOU) _____.

3. "Have you _____ to Europe?"
   (YOU) _____.

4. "Have you _____ lunch today?"
   (YOU) _____.

5. "Have you _____ your homework today?"
   (YOU) _____.

8 ▶ **Complete the conversation with the present perfect or the simple past tense. Use contractions when possible.**

Joe: _____ this tour before? I hear it's great.
          1. you / take

Trish: Yes, I have. I _____ to Russia with this group two years ago.
                      2. come

It _____ a wonderful trip. _____ here before?
  3. be   **4. you / be**

Joe: Yes, I _____ Moscow in 2002, but I _____ much of the city.
              5. visit   **6. not / see**

It _____ a business trip. I'm really excited about *this* trip!
  7. be

Trish: Me too. I _____ the brochures several times last night.
                  8. read

I can't wait to see all these places again. By the way,

_____ Peter, our tour guide?
  9. you / meet

Joe: No, but I'd like to.

Trish: Come. I'll introduce you.

LESSON 2

9 ▶ **Complete the sentences. Circle the correct words.**

1. Have you (ever / yet) visited the art museums in Paris?

2. I haven't been to the opera (already / yet).

3. Who is she? I haven't seen her (ever / before).

4. Has Evan (yet / ever) tried ceviche (before / already)?

5. We've only been here one day, but we've (already / yet) taken a lot of pictures.

6. I'm sorry. I haven't finished the job (already / yet).

7. He's only fourteen years old, but he's (already / yet) traveled all over the world.

10 ▶ **Complete each conversation. Write questions or answers in the present perfect. Use <u>ever</u>, <u>before</u>, <u>already</u>, or <u>yet</u>.**

1. A: Has Ted taken a tour of the Statue of Liberty yet?

   B: Yes. He _____.

2. A: _____?

   B: No. Actually this is my first time to London.

3. A: _____?

   B: No, but they plan to go to the top of the Sears Tower tomorrow.

4. A: Has Lisa ever tried Turkish food?

   B: Yes. She _____ several times.

11 Look at Anne Marie and Gilbert's To-Do List for their vacation in Toronto.
Anne Marie has checked what they've already done.

> ✔ – take a tour of the University
>
> ✔ – meet Michel for dinner on
>   Spadina Avenue
>
> – visit the Bata Shoe Museum
>
> ✔ – see a musical downtown
>
> – take a boat trip around Toronto Harbor
>
> ✔ – go shopping at the Eaton Centre

Now finish Anne Marie's postcard to her friend. Write what she and Gilbert have
already done and what they haven't done yet. Use the present perfect.

Dear Agnes,   Sunday, August 6

Gilbert and I are having a wonderful time in Toronto.
We've done so many things! _____

_____

_____

_____

_____

_____

_____

_____

See you when we get back.

Love,
Anne Marie

LESSON 3

 12 Read the information about greetings in Asia. Then read the statements and check <u>true</u>, <u>false</u>, or <u>no information</u>.

 GETTING GREETINGS RIGHT

The traditional greeting in Asia is a bow. In fact, there are different types of bows used in greetings throughout Asia. For example, in Japan, China, and Korea, people bow, but in Japan the bow is usually lower. In India and nearby countries in South Asia, most people put their hands together and bow just a little.

While each Asian culture has its own traditional special greeting, these days, don't be surprised if people in Asia just shake your hand.

SOURCE: www.factmonster.com and *Kiss, Bow, or Shake Hands.*

	true	false	no information
1. People in China, Japan, and Korea bow when they greet someone.	☐	☐	☐
2. In Korea, people usually bow lower than in Japan.	☐	☐	☐
3. In India, you shouldn't touch the person you are greeting.	☐	☐	☐
4. People in many places in South Asia use a similar greeting.	☐	☐	☐

13 WHAT ABOUT YOU? **Complete these sentences about yourself.**

1. In this country, the most common greeting is _____.

2. When I greet someone for the first time, I usually _____.

3. When I greet a family member or close friend, I usually _____.

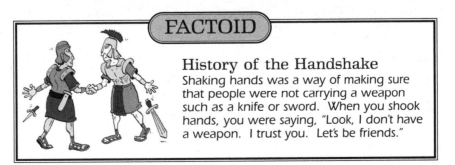

FACTOID

History of the Handshake
Shaking hands was a way of making sure that people were not carrying a weapon such as a knife or sword. When you shook hands, you were saying, "Look, I don't have a weapon. I trust you. Let's be friends."

SOURCE: www.canadaone.com

LESSON 4

14 George Ruez is a true adventurer. He has done a lot of things in his life. Write
questions about George. Use the present perfect with <u>ever</u> or <u>before</u>.

1. *Has George ever been to Paris* _____? (Paris)

2. _____? (horseback riding)

3. _____? (Mt. Everest)

4. _____? (guinea pig)

5. _____? (octopus)

6. _____? (Mt. Kilimanjaro)

7. _____? (sailing)

8. _____? (Buenos Aires)

15 Look at the pictures showing some of the things George has done.
Now answer the questions from Exercise 14. Use the present perfect
with <u>yet</u> or <u>already</u>.

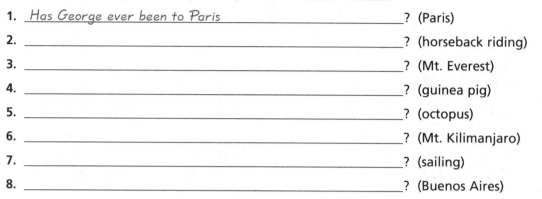

1. _____.

2. _____.

3. _____.

4. _____.

5. _____.

6. _____.

7. _____.

8. _____.

GRAMMAR BOOSTER

A **Read the first sentence. Then decide if the second sentence is true (T) or false (F).**

1. I've never been to Lebanon.   ____ I went to Lebanon a long time ago.

2. He hasn't been to Barbados yet.   ____ He was in Barbados last week.

3. She's already left for Tokyo.   ____ She is going to Tokyo.

4. She has never been to Mexico before.   ____ This is her first visit to Mexico.

5. We have visited Bangkok several times.   ____ We've been to Bangkok before.

B **Look at the answers. Write questions with <u>What</u> (OR <u>Which</u>).**

1. **A:** _____?

   B: I've tried Hungarian food and German food.

2. **A:** _____?

   B: We've been to Morocco and Egypt.

3. **A:** _____?

   B: He's gone to the Metropolitan Museum of Art and the Museum of Modern Art.

4. **A:** _____?

   B: She's studied Spanish and English.

5. **A:** _____?

   B: I've visited Budapest and Prague.

6. **A:** _____?

   B: We've seen two operas—*Carmen* and *Othello*.

C **Complete the conversation with the present perfect or the simple past tense. Use contractions when possible.**

A: Welcome to Rome! When _____ you _____?
                                                           1. arrive

B: A few days ago.

A: Oh, that's great. _____ you _____ sightseeing yet?
                                                        2. go

B: Yes, a little. I _____ Piazza Navona already and I _____ a tour of
                        3. see   **4. take**

the Coliseum yesterday.

A: Great! _____ you _____ to Vatican City yet?
                                                      5. be

B: Yes, as a matter of fact. I _____ there on Thursday.
                                        6. go

A: How about Italian food? _____ you _____ any real Italian
                                                            7. eat

pizza or pasta yet?

B: I _____ pasta with seafood last night. But I _____ any calamari yet.
       8. have   **9. not try**

I _____ so many times that's something I shouldn't miss.
     10. hear

A: Oh, yes! The calamari here is excellent. And Rome is a great city. Enjoy your stay!

B: Thanks.

D Rewrite the sentences, using the word(s) in parentheses.

1. Have you been to Taiwan? (before)

   _____?

2. Josefina hasn't had her lunch. (yet)

   _____.

3. He was born in Egypt, but he hasn't seen the pyramids. (never)

   _____.

4. Has Gus taken a tour of the city? (before)

   _____?

5. I haven't tried octopus. (never)

   _____.

6. Have you had anything to eat? (yet)

   _____?

7. Have you been to the outdoor market? (ever, before)

   _____?

8. Prague is so beautiful! I haven't been here. (never, before)

   _____.

9. She's finished college. (already)

   _____.

E WHAT ABOUT YOU? Answer the questions with sentences about yourself. Give details about your experiences.

1. "What's an unusual food you've tried?"

   YOU _____.

2. "What's an interesting country or city you've been to?"

   YOU _____.

3. "What's an exciting sport you've played?"

   YOU _____.

4. "What's a wonderful book you've read?"

   YOU _____.

JUST FOR FUN

1 ▷ FIGURE IT OUT! Rearrange the letters of the following phrase to form the name of a famous building in England. (Hint: 3 words)

ONE OLD FORT NOW

2 ▷ The drawings show gestures and customs that should or should not be used in certain countries. Unscramble the letters to form the name of each country.

1. In _____, you should never touch a person, even a child, on the head. (ADLITAHN)

2. In _____, open a gift immediately and thank the person who gave it to you. (RCEDAUO)

3. In _____, you should cover your mouth when you're using a toothpick. (AWINAT)

4. In the _____, it's better not to ask people personal questions such as how much money they make. (DTEIUN NGMIKOD) (2 words)

5. In _____, you should take off your shoes before entering someone's home. (AANPJ)

6. In _____, putting a coat on a chair in a restaurant is considered rude. (SUASIR)

Movies and Entertainment

TOPIC PREVIEW

1 ▶ **Choose the correct response. Circle the letter.**

1. "Did you see *Aliens Alive* when it came out last summer?"

   a. I'd rather watch the tube.   b. No. I missed it.

2. "I really want to see the new Jackie Chan movie. What do you say?"

   a. Have you already seen it?   b. I'm not in the mood for an action film.

3. "How about we go see a classic movie?"

   a. Deal!   b. They said it was great.

4. "Would you like some Chinese food after the movie?"

   a. Actually, I'd rather have Italian food.   b. How about it?

2 ▶ **Write the genre of the movie under the picture.**

1. _____ 2. _____ 3. _____ 4. _____ 5. _____

3 ▶ **Read the newspaper movie listings. Choose a genre that best describes each movie. Write the title of another movie of that genre you've seen.**

ESSEX TIMES

Friday, May 22   ENTERTAINMENT   page 39

The Fearless Fighter 🎥

You'll be on the edge of your seat. Don't miss this exciting adventure! But don't bring the kids—a little too violent.
—Josephine Potter, NewsNow

Edgewood Theater:
6:00, 8:15, 10:30

Myra's Day 🎥

Spend the day with Myra. You'll laugh so hard you might fall out of your seat!
—Roger Sullivan, Movietime

Plaza Cinemas:
2:00, 4:00, 6:00, 8:00, 10:00

Goodnight, Mariana 🎥

Mariana tries to find her long lost mother. Her search takes her all over the country. Very sad and touching. Based on a true story.
—Oscar Wilson, www.OWfilms.com

Castle Theater:
1:45, 4:00, 6:15, 8:30

Genre: _____   Genre: _____   Genre: _____

Movie: _____   Movie: _____   Movie: _____

WHAT ABOUT YOU? **Which of the movies from the listing in Exercise 3 would you most like to see? Why?**

LESSON 1

5 **Look at the pictures. Then complete the conversation.**

Patty: Hi, Rosemary. Sorry I'm late. Have you been here long?

Rosemary: For about twenty minutes. What happened?

Patty: Well, first _____. I ran to catch it, but it pulled away.
1.

And _____, because it was raining. So, I went back home to
2.

get my car. Then _____. Finally I got here, but _____.
3.   4.

It took me about ten minutes before I found one!

Rosemary: Well, you're here now. Let's go see the movie!

6 **Complete the posting from an online movie chat room. Use since or for.**

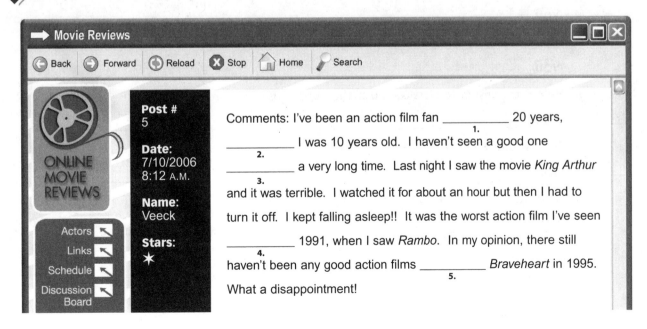

Comments: I've been an action film fan _____ 20 years,
1.
_____ I was 10 years old. I haven't seen a good one
2.
_____ a very long time. Last night I saw the movie *King Arthur*
3.
and it was terrible. I watched it for about an hour but then I had to
turn it off. I kept falling asleep!! It was the worst action film I've seen
_____ 1991, when I saw *Rambo*. In my opinion, there still
4.
haven't been any good action films _____ *Braveheart* in 1995.
5.
What a disappointment!

LESSON 2

7 Complete each statement about movie genres. Write the letter on the line.

1. Fighting and killing are common in __e__ .

2. In the past, ____ were drawn by hand, but a lot of them are now done on the computer.

3. A ____ tells a story with singing and dancing.

4. A ____ gives facts and information about real people and events.

5. A ____ usually takes place in the future.

6. *Airplane* is a great ____ . I can't stop laughing every time I watch it.

7. This courtroom ____ is a serious movie about life and death.

8. Scary things happen in ____ .

a. drama
b. documentary
c. science-fiction film
d. horror films
e. action films
f. animated films
g. musical
h. comedy

8 Look at Tom's favorite things and <u>least</u> favorite things.

Tom's Favorite Things

1. comedy
2. a trip to the beach
3. pop music
4. rice
5. going to the gym

Tom's <u>Least</u> Favorite Things

1. documentary
2. a trip to the mountains
3. classical music
4. pasta
5. going shopping

Now read each statement and circle <u>T</u> (true) or <u>F</u> (false), based on Tom's lists. Then write five true statements about yourself. Use <u>would rather</u>.

1. Tom would rather see a comedy than a documentary.   T   F

   YOU _____ .

2. He'd rather take a trip to the mountains than to the beach.   T   F

   YOU _____ .

3. He'd rather listen to classical music than pop music.   T   F

   YOU _____ .

4. Tom would rather have rice than pasta.   T   F

   YOU _____ .

5. He'd rather go to the gym than go shopping.   T   F

   YOU _____ .

LESSON 3

9 Read the online movie reviews and fill in the chart. Write the genre and choose at least two adjectives from the box that best describe the movie. Then write the name of a movie of the same genre that you've seen.

| funny | boring | silly | violent | unforgettable | weird | interesting |

The Movies

File   Edit   Links   Tools   Help   Chat

Address   www.thereviewpages.com

THE REVIEW PAGES

THE ALIEN!
I was really looking forward to this: Martians take over a city in the year 2020. I usually love these kinds of movies, but *The Alien!* is just too strange for words. The story doesn't make sense. It was downright stupid!

—Kris Baker

SEARCH FOR THE LOST KINGDOM
This is going to be a blockbuster hit! The acting was terrific! A little too much killing for me, but it was still a great movie. I won't forget this movie for a long time!

—Ajay007

DAD'S BACK!
In *Dad's Back!*, Morgan Silva documents himself and his family for a whole month. It sounds boring, but you'll be surprised at how really humorous and entertaining the movie is. I strongly recommend this film to everyone out there.

—Marty1995

DON'T SCREAM NOW
A film about a killer monster is scary and exciting, right? Not this one! It was not interesting at all! Almost everyone gets killed, and still I couldn't stay awake! I'd rather have stayed home and read a book.

—Yasir

ONLINE

Movie title	Genre	Adjectives	Similar movie I've seen
The Alien!			
Search for the Lost Kingdom			
Dad's Back!			
Don't Scream Now			

10 Complete the conversation. Write the letter on the line.

A: Hi, Janelle. Seen any good movies recently?

B: _____
1.

A: *Play Time*? What kind of movie is that?

B: _____
2.

A: Really? What is it about?

B: _____
3.

A: That doesn't sound very funny. Was it any good?

B: _____
4.

A: The funniest? Wow! Who was in it?

B: _____
5.

A: So you would recommend it?

B: _____
6.

a. It was terrific. It might be the funniest film I've seen this year.

b. It's a comedy. You have to see it.

c. Oh, yes. I think you'd like it.

d. Yeah, I just saw *Play Time* at the Art Cinema.

e. It's about some high school kids who don't want to graduate.

f. It stars Wilson Grant—he was really hilarious.

11 CHALLENGE. WHAT ABOUT YOU? Write your <u>own</u> review about a movie you've seen. Use the reviews in Exercise 9 for support. In your review, try to answer the following questions: What kind of movie was it? What was it about? Who was in it? Was it good? Would you recommend it?

LESSON 4

12 Read the article. Then complete the statements, according to the information in the article. Circle the letter.

Children and Media Violence

Did you know that according to a recent study, children spend 6½ hours with the media* every day? Between the ages of 4 and 18, the average child sees 200,000 acts of violence on TV and other media, including 40,000 murders. Another study found that 61% of television programs show some violence, and 43% of these violent scenes are used to make people laugh. Also, 44% of the time, violent people in movies seem attractive or beautiful. In other media, like video games, 60 to 90% of the most popular games have violent subject matter. Other studies show that when children and young adults watch violent movies and play violent video games, they act more violently. As a result, these children see violence as a way to work out problems.

*Media in these studies include TV, movies, cartoons, video games, and the Internet.

SOURCE: http://www.mediafamily.org

1. Between the ages of 4 and 18, the average child sees ____.

   a. 40,000 television programs   b. 200,000 murders   c. 40,000 murders on TV and in other media

2. ____ of all TV shows contain violent scenes.

   a. More than half   b. Half   c. Less than half

3. Violence on TV is often meant to be seen as ____.

   a. unforgettable   b. funny   c. scary

4. People who are violent in movies are shown as ____.

   a. good-looking   b. silly   c. dangerous

5. Viewing violent movies and playing violent video games can make people ____.

   a. more violent   b. more boring   c. more beautiful

13 WHAT ABOUT YOU? Complete the Violence in the Media Survey.

Violence in the Media Survey

1. Do you think there is too much violence in the media?   ☐ YES   ☐ NO

2. What types of media do you think show the most violence?

   _____

3. What kinds of TV shows and movies do you spend the most time watching? Rank these from 1 (most watched) to 8 (least watched).

   ☐ dramas
   ☐ comedies
   ☐ cartoons
   ☐ action
   ☐ music videos
   ☐ horror
   ☐ documentaries
   ☐ other   Please specify: _____

4. How many TV shows and movies that you see each week contain violent acts?

   ☐ 0–5
   ☐ 5–10
   ☐ 10–15
   ☐ 15–20
   ☐ over 20

5. I think that watching violent TV shows and movies . . .

   ☐ makes people more likely to act violently themselves.
   ☐ makes people less likely to behave violently themselves.
   ☐ has no effect on people's behavior.

GRAMMAR BOOSTER

A Fill in the chart with the correct forms of the irregular verbs.

Base Form	Simple Past Tense	Past Participle	Present Participle
be	was / were	been	being
	ate		
go			
			having
		heard	
	met		
sit			
			speaking
take			
		written	
	paid		
			making

B Read the first sentence. Then decide if the second sentence is true (<u>T</u>) or false (<u>F</u>).

1. She's been living in Milan for two years.　　　____ She still lives in Milan.

2. She's lived in Milan for two years.　　　____ She no longer lives in Milan.

3. I've been renting a lot of DVDs lately.　　　____ I am still renting DVDs.

4. How long have you been watching that film?　　　____ You are still watching the film.

5. She's written a review of the new movie.　　　____ She's finished writing the review.

6. We've been waiting to see *Black Cat, White Cat*.　　　____ We have already seen *Black Cat, White Cat*.

C WHAT ABOUT YOU? Answer the questions. Use your <u>own</u> words.

1. "How long have you been studying English?"

   YOU _____.

2. "How long have you lived in this city or town?"

   YOU _____.

3. "Is there any movie you've been waiting to see?"

   YOU _____.

D Read about U.S. tennis star Serena Williams. Underline all the verbs in the present perfect. Circle all the time expressions with <u>since</u> or <u>for</u>.

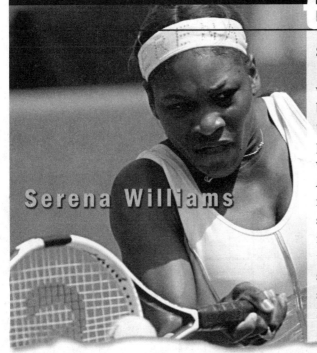

tennis

Serena Williams

Serena Williams was born on September 26, 1981. She picked up her first tennis racket when she was four. Since then she has become one of the greatest tennis players in the world. Born in Michigan in the central part of the U.S., she moved to California when she was two. She has lived in Los Angeles for most of her life. She played her first tournament at age eight. Since then she has won many international competitions, including Wimbledon, the U.S. Open, and the Australian Open. She is handling her success well. Since she turned professional, she has played tennis all over the world and has earned millions of dollars.

 Complete the interview about Serena Williams, using the present perfect or the present perfect continuous. Use the present perfect continuous only if the action is continuous or unfinished. Then answer the questions with information from Exercise D.

1. How long / she / play tennis?

   Q: _____?

   A: _____.

2. How long / she / live in California?

   Q: _____?

   A: _____.

3. she / win any competitions / since her first tournament?

   Q: _____?

   A: _____.

4. How much money / she / earn / since she began her career?

   Q: _____?

   A: _____.

JUST FOR FUN

1 ▶ Read the clues and complete the crossword puzzle.

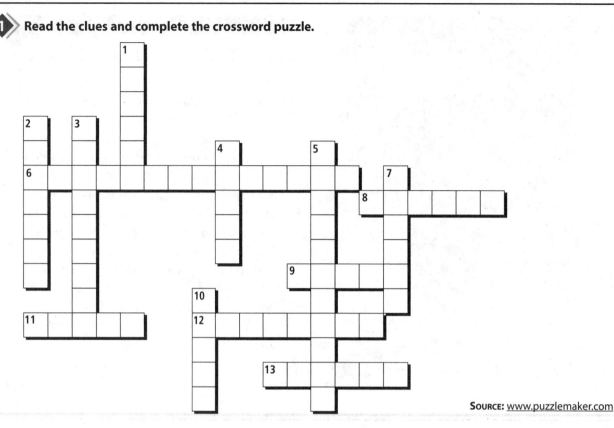

SOURCE: www.puzzlemaker.com

Across

6. movies that usually take place in the future
8. very scary film
9. very strange
11. another word for *hilarious*
12. about love
13. not interesting

Down

1. movie with a lot of fighting and killing
2. movie with singing and dancing
3. hand-drawn or computer-generated characters and scenery
4. not serious; almost stupid
5. movie about real-life events
7. movie that makes you laugh
10. serious movie, not funny

2 ▶ Fill in the answers.

1. When you really feel like doing something, you are in the ◯__ __ __.
2. Another name for the TV is the ◯__ __◯.
3. If something is hilarious, it's very __ __◯◯__.
4. When you're stuck in ◯__ __ __ ◯__, you're usually late.
5. The place where you go to see a movie is called the ◯__◯__ __ ◯.
6. An old movie is sometimes called a __ __◯__ __ __ __.
7. Another word for a type of movie is a __◯◯__ __.

Now unscramble the circled letters. What's the new word? _____

Answer: entertainment

18 UNIT 2

UNIT 3

Staying at Hotels

TOPIC PREVIEW

1 Look at the hotel bill. Then answer the questions.

```
  Mr. Philip Paul              ROOM      1631
  11 Rue Ravignan              ARRIVAL   09/14            NOVA
  Place Emil Goudeau           DEPARTURE 09/16            HOTEL
  75018 Paris, France          TIME      15:52
  CLUB ONE MEMBER # PP2139
```

DATE	REFERENCE	DESCRIPTION	AMOUNT
9/14	13:13	Local Call	Free (Club One member)
9/14	08:32	Overseas Call	40.34
9/14	3036	Internet access	Free (Club One member)
9/14	2765	Laundry	36.00
9/14		Room 1631	179.00
9/14	3036	Internet access	Free (Club One member)
9/14	2762	Room Service	18.92
9/15	2762	Room Service	26.45
9/15	09:52	Local Call	Free (Club One member)
9/15	428	Photocopies	Free (Club One member)
9/15	3036	Internet access	Free (Club One member)
9/15	758	Local Fax	Free (Club One member)
9/15		Room 1631	179.00
9/15	09562	Airport Shuttle	30.00

	BALANCE	509.71
	VAT 7.00%	35.68
	TOTAL INCLUDING VAT	545.39

1. What date did Mr. Paul check in? _____

2. How much did he pay for phone calls, faxes, and Internet usage? _____

3. What other hotel services did he use? _____

4. How much is the tax? _____

2 What hotel services were most important to Mr. Paul? Circle the hotel services he used more than once. Underline the services he did not use at all.

Internet access   telephone   airport shuttle   minibar

wake-up service   laundry   room service

3 WHAT ABOUT YOU? Which hotel services are important to you? Complete the paragraph.

The most important hotel service for me is _____ because

_____ . Of course, _____ is also an important

service, but _____ is not important to me at all. I can live without it!

4 Read the Nova Hotel's Club One brochure. Then read the statements and check <u>true</u> or <u>false</u>.

CLUB ONE

Club One is our special member program available to you. You don't have to pay a fee to join Club One. It's free! As a Club One member, just pick up your key at the desk, and your room is prepared exactly as you wish. We'll have a welcome beverage and snack waiting for you there at no charge. And you'll receive a 10% discount on all room service orders. We offer many other member specials, including free local phone calls, free fax, free copies, and free high-speed Internet access. Become a member today!

	true	false
1. You have to pay to join Club One.	☐	☐
2. Club One members get some free food and drinks in their rooms.	☐	☐
3. Room service is free for Club One members.	☐	☐
4. Internet access is not free for Club One members.	☐	☐
5. Club One members can make local phone calls for free.	☐	☐

LESSON 1

5 Put the conversation in order. Write the number on the line.

_1_ Can I speak with Kevin Mercer, please? He's staying in room 376.

____ That's right.

____ Yes. Could you tell him Barbara called? Please ask him to call me back at 31–56–97.

____ One moment, please . . . I'm sorry. There's no answer. Can I take a message?

____ Barbara at 31–56–97?

____ Is that all?

_7_ Yes, that's it. Thank you very much.

6 ► **Choose the best response. Circle the letter.**

1. "Is Rosa Mayall in?"

   a. Too bad.   **b.** I'd love to.   **c.** Yes, just a moment please.

2. "When will she be back?"

   a. In an hour.   **b.** Yesterday.   **c.** Tell her I called.

3. "Can I leave her a message?"

   a. Not yet.   **b.** Sure.   **c.** No, thanks. I'll call back later.

7 ► **The fortune-teller is predicting the future. Read her predictions. Then rewrite the sentences, using <u>will</u>.**

1. _____.

2. _____.

3. _____.

4. _____.

5. _____.

FACTOID: TELEPHONES

There are more than 600 million telephone lines today, yet almost half the world's population has never made a phone call.

Source: www.didyouknow.cd

8 ▸ **Read the phone conversation. Then complete the message sheet.**

A: Hello. I'd like to speak with Ms. Marina Santiago, please.

B: One moment, please. I'll ring Ms. Santiago's room . . . I'm sorry, but there's no answer. Would you like to call back later?

A: No, I'd like to leave a message. Please tell her that Anna Streed called. I'll be at 555–8723 until 5:00 today.

B: OK, Ms. Anna Street . . .

A: No, it's Streed, S-T-R-E-E-D— that's D as in "door."

B: Oh, OK, Ms. Anna Streed, 555–8723. I'll make sure she gets the message.

A: Thank you.

To _Marina Santiago_

Date ___9/14___   Time ___3:15___   A.M. ☐
P.M. ☒

WHILE YOU WERE OUT

☐ Mr./ ☐ Ms./ ☐ Mrs. _____

Phone _____
Area code   Number   Extension

☐ telephoned   ☐ please call
☐ returned your call   ☐ will call back

Message: _____
_____

LESSON 2

9 ▸ **Complete the conversation. Write the letter on the line.**

A: Hello. I'm checking in. The name is Chang, Ken Chang.

B: ____
1.

A: Actually, I don't need a suite. It's just me, so a single room will be fine.

B: ____
2.

A: Smoking, please. Does the room have Internet access?

B: ____
3.

A: That's great. Thanks.

B: ____
4.

A: Here's my credit card.

B: ____
5.

a. No problem. Would you like a smoking or non-smoking room?

b. Thank you.

c. Yes, sir. That's a suite with a king-size bed, right?

d. You're welcome. And how do you want to pay?

e. Yes, all the rooms in the hotel have free wireless Internet access.

10 CHALLENGE. Choose appropriate hotel room features for each person or group.

1. Mr. and Mrs. Benson, traveling alone:

   a single room with a king-size bed

2. Jon and Marie Smith with their two young children:

   _____

3. Mrs. Wu, with her husband, her two sons, and her mother:

   _____

4. Laura Cole, planning to have meetings in her hotel room:

   _____

5. Nicole Maxwell and her five-year-old daughter:

   _____

6. Julio Chavez, traveling alone on business:

   _____

11 Look at the pictures and complete the sentences with **'d better** or **'d better not**.

1. Hey, look at that sign. We _____

   _____

   _____.

2. Blackbird is a very popular restaurant.

   You _____

   _____.

3. It's after midnight. We _____

   _____

   _____.

4. The movie starts in three minutes.

   You _____

   _____.

LESSON 3

12 **Label the pictures.**

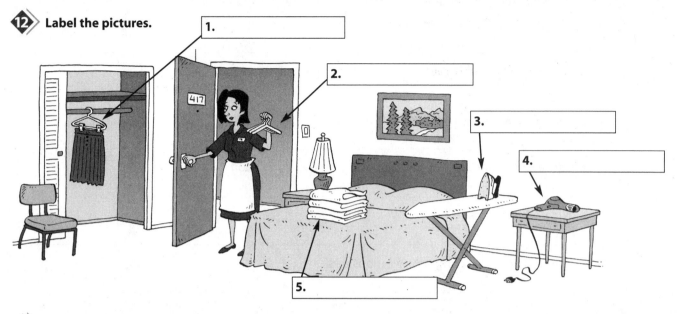

1. _____

2. _____

3. _____

4. _____

5. _____

13 **Look at the pictures. Then complete the conversations.**

1. **A:** Guest services. May I help you?

   B: Yes, please. Could you bring up some

   _____?

   A: Certainly.

   B: And I could use a _____, too.
   My hair is wet, and I don't see one in the bathroom.

   A: Sure. We'll bring those up right away.
   Anything else?

   B: Oh, yes. I have a lot of dirty clothes. Could

   someone please _____?

   A: Yes, of course.

   B: I think that's all. Thanks!

2. **A:** Front Desk. May I help you?

   B: Yes, I'd like to go for a swim. Is the

   _____ still open?

   A: No, I'm sorry, it closed at 9:00.

   B: Oh. Well, maybe a workout. How about the

   _____?

   A: No, it also just closed.

   B: Oh, no. Well, I guess I'll have to do some work then.

   Is the _____ still open?

   A: No, I'm sorry, it closed at 6:30. But you do
   have high-speed Internet access in your room.

   B: Oh, OK. Thanks.

24 **UNIT 3**

LESSON 4

 Read the online articles. Then answer the questions below, according to the information in the articles.

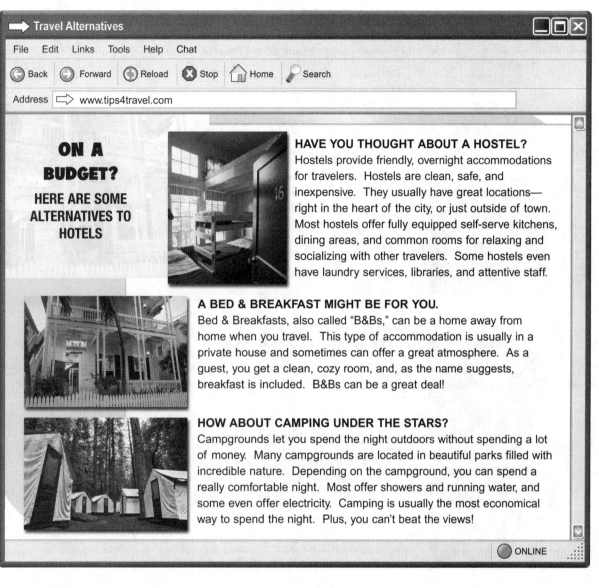

ON A BUDGET?

HERE ARE SOME ALTERNATIVES TO HOTELS

HAVE YOU THOUGHT ABOUT A HOSTEL?

Hostels provide friendly, overnight accommodations for travelers. Hostels are clean, safe, and inexpensive. They usually have great locations—right in the heart of the city, or just outside of town. Most hostels offer fully equipped self-serve kitchens, dining areas, and common rooms for relaxing and socializing with other travelers. Some hostels even have laundry services, libraries, and attentive staff.

A BED & BREAKFAST MIGHT BE FOR YOU.

Bed & Breakfasts, also called "B&Bs," can be a home away from home when you travel. This type of accommodation is usually in a private house and sometimes can offer a great atmosphere. As a guest, you get a clean, cozy room, and, as the name suggests, breakfast is included. B&Bs can be a great deal!

HOW ABOUT CAMPING UNDER THE STARS?

Campgrounds let you spend the night outdoors without spending a lot of money. Many campgrounds are located in beautiful parks filled with incredible nature. Depending on the campground, you can spend a really comfortable night. Most offer showers and running water, and some even offer electricity. Camping is usually the most economical way to spend the night. Plus, you can't beat the views!

1. Which is usually the cheapest type of accommodation? _____

2. Which type of accommodation has a kitchen? _____

3. Where can you always get breakfast? _____

4. Where can you probably use your computer? _____

5. Where might you be able to wash clothes? _____

6. Where should you stay if you like to meet new people? _____

7. Which type of accommodation is best for you if you like hiking and fishing?

   _____

CHALLENGE. Read the statements. Which accommodation is best for each of these people, based on the online articles in Exercise 14? Give advice, using <u>had better (not)</u> or <u>should (not)</u>.

I'm a student, and I like to meet new and interesting people when I travel.

1. He should _____

_____.

Peter always wants to save money, but on vacation, I like a comfortable bed and some privacy.

2. They _____

_____.

Location is everything to me. I've got to be close to the clubs and shops.

3. _____

_____.

I'd rather spend my vacation in the countryside than sightseeing in the city. Comfort's not so important to me.

4. _____

_____.

16 **WHAT ABOUT YOU? Which type of accommodation is best for you? Why? Complete the paragraph.**

I would like to stay

GRAMMAR BOOSTER

A Complete the sentences, using <u>will</u> or <u>won't</u>.
Use contractions when possible.

A: _____ you be staying with us another night?
1.

B: No, we _____. But I think we _____ be back
2.   3.

next month.

A: Great. How _____ you be paying today?
4.

B: I _____ use my credit card, if that's OK.
5.

A: Sure. That _____ be fine.
6.

B Look at the pictures. What do you think the man is going to do?
Write sentences with a form of <u>be going to</u> or <u>not be going to</u>.

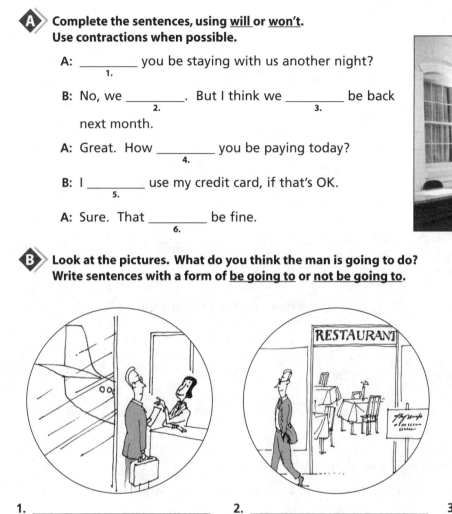

1. _____

_____

2. _____

_____

3. _____

_____

4. _____

_____

5. _____

_____

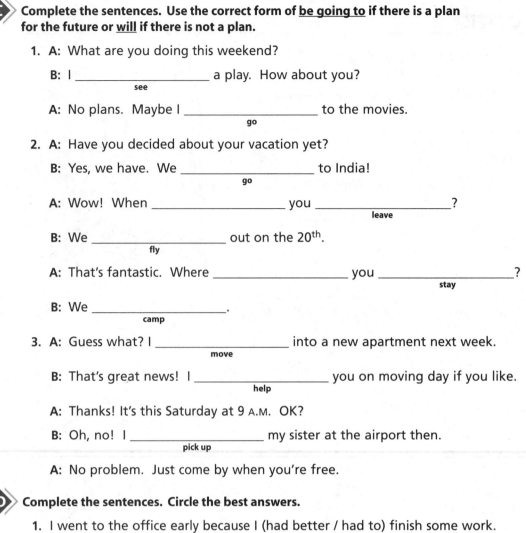

C Complete the sentences. Use the correct form of <u>be going to</u> if there is a plan for the future or <u>will</u> if there is not a plan.

1. **A:** What are you doing this weekend?

   B: I _____ a play. How about you?
   _{see}

   A: No plans. Maybe I _____ to the movies.
   _{go}

2. **A:** Have you decided about your vacation yet?

   B: Yes, we have. We _____ to India!
   _{go}

   A: Wow! When _____ you _____?
   _{leave}

   B: We _____ out on the 20th.
   _{fly}

   A: That's fantastic. Where _____ you _____?
   _{stay}

   B: We _____.
   _{camp}

3. **A:** Guess what? I _____ into a new apartment next week.
   _{move}

   B: That's great news! I _____ you on moving day if you like.
   _{help}

   A: Thanks! It's this Saturday at 9 A.M. OK?

   B: Oh, no! I _____ my sister at the airport then.
   _{pick up}

   A: No problem. Just come by when you're free.

D Complete the sentences. Circle the best answers.

1. I went to the office early because I (had better / had to) finish some work.

2. You (must not / don't have to) tell Linda about the surprise party. It's a secret.

3. You have a lot of homework. You really (ought to / could) get started.

4. We (were supposed to / had better) be at the airport by now! I hope we don't miss our plane!

5. I don't think this restaurant accepts credit cards. (Could / Must) we pay by check?

JUST FOR FUN

1 WORD FIND. Look at the pictures. The words are across (→), down (↓), diagonal (↘), and sometimes backwards (←). Circle the six hotel services. Then write the hotel services on the lines.

O	R	C	N	Q	Y	Z	B	S	S	N	B
B	R	A	T	L	L	F	H	T	Y	O	E
B	A	O	B	S	A	O	X	F	H	Z	L
G	Y	B	B	I	E	A	G	R	Q	Y	L
R	B	U	Y	S	N	V	J	G	N	W	S
S	B	C	H	S	R	I	B	A	F	L	E
S	G	I	J	W	I	X	M	T	U	S	R
C	N	Y	E	H	S	T	L	X	O	U	V
E	Y	Q	Y	C	T	X	T	D	Q	Z	I
R	O	O	M	S	E	R	V	I	C	E	C
Y	R	D	N	U	A	L	C	I	N	Z	E
P	R	M	E	O	X	O	X	Y	U	G	U

SOURCE: Created by Puzzlemaker at <u>DiscoverySchool.com</u>

_____   _____

_____   _____

_____   _____

2 TAKE A GUESS! Which of these hotels actually exists? After you guess, read the information at the bottom of the page.

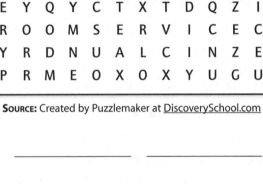

SOURCE: www.jul.com

Underseal Lodge remains on duty 24 hours a day to provide whatever services the guests may need.

hotel. Guests must scuba dive 21 feet, or 6.5 meters, beneath the surface of the sea to check in! The staff of Jules'

Answer to Exercise 2: It's the third one. "Jules' Undersea Lodge" in Key Largo, Florida is the world's only underwater

Staying at Hotels **29**

UNIT 4

Cars and Driving

TOPIC PREVIEW

1 ▶ Read the conversation. Then complete the rental request.

AGENT: Hi. How can I help you?

RENTER: Hello. I'd like to make a reservation for June 20th.

AGENT: Certainly. Let's see . . . There's a Fiat Siena available.

RENTER: Is it air-conditioned?

AGENT: No, I'm sorry, it isn't. I have a Renault Clio that is.

RENTER: That'll be great.

AGENT: How long do you need the car for?

RENTER: For eight days.

AGENT: No problem. You can pick the car up in the afternoon at L & M Car Rental's main office downtown.

RENTER: And do I drop it off there, too?

AGENT: No, you have to drop it off at the airport, no later than 3 P.M.

RENTER: OK, that's fine.

AGENT: Can you please fill this out . . .

L & M Car Rental Agency, Ltd.

Pickup date / time: _____

Pickup location: _____

Return date / time: _____

Return location: _____

Car type: _____

---

2 ▶ Choose the correct response. Circle the letter.

1. "How can I help you?"

   a. No, thanks.   b. I have a reservation.   c. Certainly, sir.

2. "Do you need an automatic transmission or manual?"

   a. That's correct.   b. Oh, yes.   c. Either way.

3. "Can I see your driver's license?"

   a. Here you go.   b. No, I don't.   c. Here are the keys.

4. "Is that OK?"

   a. Good morning.   b. That'll be fine.   c. I have a reservation.

30

3 Label the car parts.

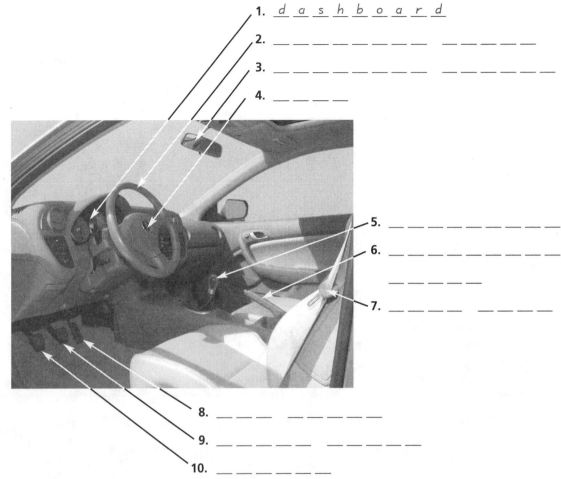

1. _d_ _a_ _s_ _h_ _b_ _o_ _a_ _r_ _d_

2. _ _ _ _ _ _ _ _   _ _ _ _ _

3. _ _ _ _ _ _ _   _ _ _ _ _ _

4. _ _ _ _ _

5. _ _ _ _ _ _ _ _ _ _ _

6. _ _ _ _ _ _ _ _ _ _

   _ _ _ _ _

7. _ _ _ _   _ _ _ _ _

8. _ _ _ _   _ _ _ _ _ _ _

9. _ _ _ _ _ _   _ _ _ _ _ _

10. _ _ _ _ _ _ _

4 Choose the correct response. Write the letter on the line.

1. "I had an accident today." ____

2. "Are you OK?" ____

3. "How did it happen?" ____

4. "Luckily, I was wearing my seat belt." ____

5. "Was there much damage?" ____

a. The other driver was speeding.

b. Not really. The other driver will have to replace a taillight.

c. Thank goodness.

d. Yes, I'm OK. No one was hurt.

e. How awful.

• FACTOID •
WHY DO PEOPLE RENT CARS?

Most cars rented are rented for vacations (66%). About one in five (21%) cars are rented for business reasons. One-tenth (10%) are rented for a combination of business and pleasure travel.

SOURCE: www.traveldailynews.com

5 Complete the conversation. Use the simple past tense or the past continuous.

A: Hi Sandra. What's wrong?

B: I _____ an accident on the way home today.
   1. have

A: Oh, no! How _____ it _____?
                2. happen

B: Well, I _____ home when my sister
          3. drive

_____. She _____ what I
   4. call   5. ask

_____, and I _____ her
   6. do   7. tell

I _____ home and would see her soon.
   8. go

But she _____ she had a funny story that
        9. say

she just <u>had</u> to tell me. Anyway, by the end of the story, I _____ so hard
                                                                    10. laugh

I couldn't see—and I _____ right into a stop sign.
                      11. drive

6 WHAT ABOUT YOU? **Have you or has someone you know ever had an accident? What happened? Write a note to a friend about it.**

LESSON 2

7 Look at the pictures. Write the letter of the correct picture after each phrasal verb.

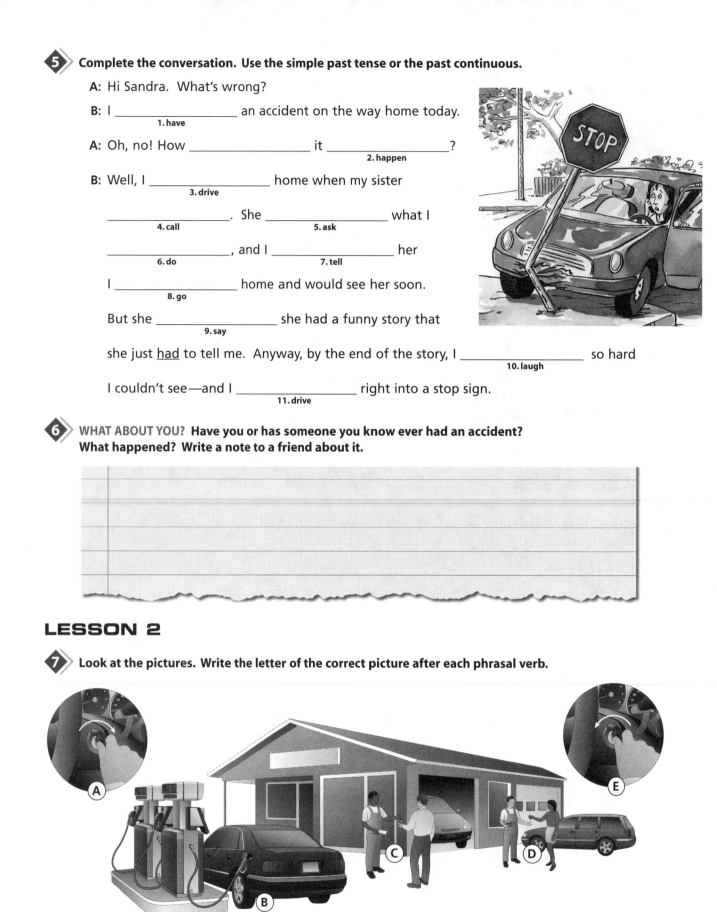

1. fill up ____   **2.** turn on ____   **3.** drop off ____   **4.** turn off ____   **5.** pick up ____

8 ▷ CHALLENGE. **Complete the note below. Use the correct phrasal verb from Exercise 7. Sometimes you will need to use direct object pronouns.**

> Hi, Lisa!
>
> I made an appointment to have Stan fix the car today. Can you _____ at the
>   1.
>
> service station this afternoon? Tell Stan that the left turn signal isn't working. This morning I could
>
> _____ , but now it's stuck, and I can't seem to _____ .
>   2.   3.
>
> Ask him to call me when the car is done. I'll _____ on my way home from work.
>   4.
>
> Love, Daniel
>
> P.S. While you're there, could you _____ the tank? See you tonight!
>   5.

9 ▷ **Choose the correct response. Circle the letter.**

1. "It'll be $9.00 to dry-clean this dress."

   a. OK. When can I pick it up?   **b.** Fill it up, please.   **c.** How about noon?

2. "Fill it up with regular, please."

   a. Sure. I'll see you at 10:00.   **b.** Yes, that's all.   **c.** Yes, ma'am. Anything else?

3. "Your computer is working. But it looks like the printer won't turn on."

   a. Yes, sir.   **b.** Can you fix it?   **c.** Terrific! I'll see you then.

4. "The seat belt on the passenger side is stuck. Can you take a look for me?"

   a. No, thanks.   **b.** That's great!   **c.** Sure. Can you drop off the car at 3:00?

LESSON 3

10 ▷ **Choose the best answer from the box to complete each sentence. Use each phrase only once.**

a convertible   a van   an SUV   a luxury car   a compact car

1. Mrs. Jeter drives _____ to take her husband to work and their five children to school every morning.

2. If you just need a car that's small and easy to park, _____ would be great for you.

3. Mavis loves hiking. She has _____ with four-wheel drive that she can drive on rough roads when she takes a trip to the mountains.

4. Peter thinks that owning _____ is really cool. He said, "You can have the roof down and enjoy the sun, wind, and beautiful sky when the weather is nice."

5. Jack is the president of a big company and he drives _____ with expensive leather seats.

11 Read the ads for three cars. Then choose the best answer to each question, according to the ads. Circle the letter.

The Ramuno is really inexpensive, and you'll find it easier than ever to own one today. You can start saving money because it's good on gas. You can even save time parking when you drive a Ramuno—with the Ramuno's size, you'll never have to worry if you can only find a tight parking spot.

RAMUNO

Love outdoor adventures? Feel the power of the four-wheel drive Vicic. It'll take you just about anywhere. The new design allows you to enjoy a comfortable ride even on the toughest mountain roads. Come test-drive it today!

Zatec You'll be amazed by how the Zatec provides comfortable seating for nine people and still has plenty of cargo room. Whether it's a few suitcases for your family's road trip or all the bags from a long day's shopping at the mall, you won't have any problem fitting them all in.

1. Which of the three cars can take the most passengers?

   a. the Vicic   **b.** the Zatec   **c.** the Ramuno

2. What do you think the Zatec is?

   a. a sports car   **b.** a full-size car   **c.** a van

3. Which of the three cars is most likely a compact car?

   a. the Ramuno   **b.** the Vicic   **c.** the Zatec

12 CHALLENGE. Which of the three cars is best for each person? Give suggestions, based on the information in the ads in Exercise 11. Explain your reasons.

1. Bryan is planning a cross-country road trip with his girlfriend. They want to do a lot of sightseeing in the countryside and go hiking in the mountains.

   _____

2. Rachel's got four kids, and she works part time. She has a lot of driving to do between work, the kids, and shopping. And she needs to carry a lot of things around.

   _____

3. Danny recently graduated from college and has just started working. He doesn't have a lot of money. He's single and lives by himself. His office is on a busy street downtown, far away from where he lives. He plans to drive to work.

   _____

13 WHAT ABOUT YOU? Have you ever rented a car? If not, would you like to? What kind of car would you like to rent, and why?

LESSON 4

(14) **Read the rental car safety tips and the information about driving in Luxembourg.**

RENTING A CAR?

Safety Tips for a Safe Drive

Driving an unfamiliar car in an unfamiliar city can be stressful and dangerous. But if you follow these tips, you'll be fine. Before you leave the rental car lot, be sure you know how to work the headlights and how to turn on and off all the signals and the interior light. Make sure everything is working properly. You should check the windshield wipers to make sure they work, too. Adjust the seat and mirrors so that you are comfortable and can see other cars around you on the road. Check the seat belts: Is there one for every passenger? Are they easy to use? And finally, if you like to listen to the radio as you drive, tune in a local station that meets your tastes. You avoid a lot of accidents, and a lot of stress, if you take care of everything before you hit the road.

Tips for Driving in Luxembourg

Make sure you Drive Alive! Always wear your seat belt!

Be careful when passing another car— always signal and allow plenty of space between you and the car in front.

Everyone in the car must wear seat belts at all times.

Don't speed! Speed limits are enforced. Speeding and other traffic violations can end in a fine, which can sometimes be a lot of money.

Don't worry about having money handy when you drive. You don't have to pay tolls to drive on any roads in Luxembourg.

SOURCE: www.driving.drive-alive.co.uk
IMAGE: budgetstockphoto.com

Complete each sentence. Circle the letter.

1. Driving a rental car can be stressful because ____.

    a. the car is dangerous   b. it's not your car   c. you don't speak the language

2. You should check the seat belts ____.

    a. before you leave the   b. before you get on   c. while you're driving
       rental car lot   the highway

3. In Luxembourg, seat belts must be worn ____.

    a. by the driver only   b. by children only   c. by everyone in the car

4. If you drive too fast in Luxembourg, you'll have to ____.

    a. talk to the police   b. pay a lot of money   c. leave the country

15 WHAT ABOUT YOU? **What helpful hints would you give someone driving in your country for the first time? Use the ideas below to write a "Drive Alive" website for your country.**

Tips for driving in _____

Make sure you Drive Alive! Always _____!

Traffic laws: _____
_____

Customs: _____
_____

Local driving habits: _____
_____

Other: _____
_____

ONLINE

GRAMMAR BOOSTER

A Complete each sentence, using the simple past tense or the past continuous.

1. They were having dinner when _____.

2. While _____, it started to rain.

3. While Marie was watching TV, her husband _____.

4. When _____, I was leaving my office.

5. He had an accident while _____.

B Rewrite the sentences in reported speech.

1. He said, "I'm leaving early today."

   He said he was leaving early today _____.

2. She said, "I'm working really hard on the project."

   _____.

3. I told him, "We're eating dinner at 8:00."

   _____.

4. They said, "It's raining outside."

   _____.

5. He told her, "They're studying at the library this evening."

   _____.

C Look at the pictures. Write a story about what happened, using the words and phrases.

drive	run in front of	hit
talk on cell phone	stop	hurt
not pay attention		damage

D Put the words in order and write sentences. If a sentence can be written in two ways, write it both ways.

1. dropped / Margo / off / the car

   Margo dropped off the car. OR Margo dropped the car off   .

2. up / it / Sam / picked

   _____.

3. the tank / filled / I / up

   _____.

4. can't / turn / on / Sue / the headlights

   _____.

5. turn / off / I / can't / them

   _____.

6. like / He'd / it / to / drop / off / at noon

   _____.

7. I / to / need / up / it / fill

   _____.

8. picked / the car / already / William / up / has

   _____.

JUST FOR FUN

1 ▶ FIGURE IT OUT! **Figure out the riddles. Read the clue and write the car part.**

1. You turn this on to let other drivers know you are turning right or left.

　□ □ □ □ □ □
　　　 4　　 5

2. When it's raining, you turn these on.

　□ □ □ □ □ □ □ □　□ □ □ □ □ □
　　　　 6　　　　　　　　　　　 3

3. You press this down to make the car go faster.

　□ □ □　□ □ □ □ □
　　　 7　　　 2

4. You look into this to see what is behind you.

　□ □ □ □ □ □ □ □　□ □ □ □ □ □
　　　　 8　　　　　　　 1

5. You push this in to move the gearshift in a manual transmission car.

　□ □ □ □ □ □
　　 9

What's the title?

□ □ □ □　□ □ □　□ □ □ □ □ □ □
9 5 3 7　5 6 2　2 3 1 8 1 6 4

2 ▶ TAKE A GUESS! **Read these unusual driving rules and regulations. Check true or false. After you finish, check your answers.**

	true	false
1. Because the streets were so crowded, Julius Caesar made a law stating that chariots could not travel in Rome during the day.	□	□
2. In ancient times, if a driver in Athens was dirty or poorly dressed, the police could refuse to let that person drive.	□	□
3. Most European countries drive on the right because when Napoleon entered these countries, he said they had to drive vehicles the same way that the French did.	□	□
4. You must drive on the right through the English Channel Tunnel (also known as the Eurotunnel or Chunnel).	□	□

Answers to Exercise 2: All of the statements are true except the last one. You don't drive in the Eurotunnel. When you arrive at the terminal, you park your car on a train wagon, and the train takes you across. When you get off the train at the other end, you get your car and then you have to choose the correct side of the road to drive on—right in France, left in England.

Personal Care and Appearance

TOPIC PREVIEW

1 Complete each conversation. Choose the correct response. Circle the letter.

I have to pick up something for my wife's birthday later. Feel like helping me?

a. I'll just go myself.

b. Sure. No problem.

(1)

I'm nervous about making the presentation at the meeting tomorrow.

a. Don't worry. You'll be fine.

b. Wish me luck.

(2)

I have to get to the office. I'm expecting an important call at three.

a. OK. See you back at the office.

b. I don't have much time today.

(3)

I'm going out for dinner later. Want to come with me?

a. It'll be a piece of cake.

b. I'm sorry. I think I'll pass.

(4)

2 Read these people's statements. Think of at least two products each person might buy at a drugstore. Write the names of the products on their shopping bags.

1. _____

2. _____

3. _____

"The dentist said I needed to take better care of my teeth."

"I just got back from the salon. I really want to try out some of the products they use there!"

"I feel terrible! I'd better get something for this cold."

3 ▷ WHAT ABOUT YOU? **What type of products do you usually buy? Rank the categories from 1 to 4 (1 = buy often, 2 = buy sometimes, 3 = don't buy often, 4 = almost never buy). Then use the prompts to complete the paragraph about your favorite product.**

_____ Hair care   _____ Tooth care   _____ Skin care   _____ Shaving   _____ Makeup

My favorite _____ product is _____.
                    (hair care / tooth care / skin care / shaving / makeup)

I buy it at _____ about _____. I especially
                    (name of store)   (how often?)

like _____ because _____
              (brand)

_____.

LESSON 1

4 ▷ **Look at the responses. Write the questions or statements to complete the conversation.**

A: _____?
                                          1.

B: Nail clippers? Did you look in aisle three?

A: _____.
                                          2.

B: I'm sorry. Let me have a look in the back. . . . I'm sorry. We're out of them.

A: _____?
                                          3.

B: Yes, the nail files should be right over here. Here you go.

A: _____.
                                          4.

B: You're very welcome.

5 ▷ **Complete the sentences. Circle the correct words.**

1. This store doesn't have (much / many) combs.

2. I can't find (some / any) sunscreen, but here's (some / any) body lotion.

3. Do you have (much / a lot of) razor blades at home?

4. She doesn't have (much / many) hair spray left.

5. Emma needs (some / any) dental floss.

6. Helen doesn't need (some / much) soap.

7. Do you have (any / many) shaving cream?

8. I have (some / any) extra shampoo.

9. I found a razor, but there aren't (some / any) razor blades here.

6 Complete the word webs. Write products or categories on the lines.

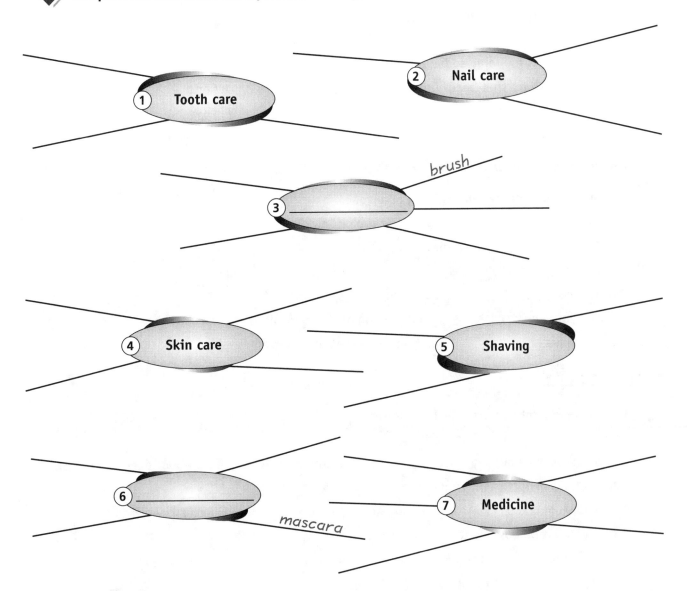

LESSON 2

7 Complete the conversation. Write the letter on the line.

A: I have an appointment for a facial with Paula.

B: _____
1.

A: Can I get a manicure in the meantime?

B: _____
2.

A: No, thanks. Actually, I'd love a cup of tea.

B: _____
3.

A: Thanks. How long will I have to wait?

B: _____
4.

a. Yes, but someone's ahead of you. Can I get you some coffee?

b. Not long. Just a few minutes.

c. I'm sorry. She's running a little late.

d. Certainly. . . . Here you go.

8 ▸ **Fill in the answers.**

1. My hair is dirty. I need a ___ ___ ___ ___ ___ (◯) ___ .

2. Your fingernails look great. When did you get your ___ ___ (◯) ___ ___ ___ ___ ___ ?

3. His hair was too long, so he got a ___ (◯) ___ ___ ___ ___ ___ .

4. I don't care for that beard on you. You should go to the barber and get a (◯) ___ ___ ___ ___ .

5. Do you have a different color nail ___ ___ (◯) ___ ___ ___ ? I'd prefer pink.

Now unscramble the circled letters. What's the new word? _____

9 ▸ **Complete each sentence with someone or anyone.**

1. I know _____ who works at the salon downtown.

2. Can _____ help me?

3. I'm sorry. We don't have _____ available to help you now.

4. There's _____ ahead of you. Can you wait?

5. Did you meet _____ interesting at the hair salon?

6. There isn't _____ waiting for you at the reception desk.

LESSON 3

10 ▸ **Choose the correct response. Circle the letter.**

1. "How long will I have to wait?"

   a. This is our slow day.　　b. I don't think so.　　c. About twenty minutes.

2. "Can I charge it to my room?"

   a. Cash or credit?　　b. Sure. No problem.　　c. Ten percent.

3. "Would it be possible to get a pedicure, too?"

   a. I think so. Let me check.　　b. How can I help you?　　c. I guess I'll wait.

4. "How much do you charge for a haircut?"

   a. Yes, you can charge it.　　b. Short hair is €35, and €45 for long hair.　　c. About thirty-five minutes.

5. "Can I possibly get a shave and a haircut? I don't have an appointment."

   a. I don't mind waiting.　　b. I think I'll pass.　　c. I'm sorry. We're fully booked.

6. "Is it customary to leave a tip for a massage?"

   a. Yes, about 15 percent of the total.　　b. That'll be fine.　　c. She can see you in ten minutes.

Look at the pictures. Check all the sentences that are true, according to the pictures.

1. ☐ **a.** Rosa is going into the salon.
   ☐ **b.** Rosa has an appointment.
   ☐ **c.** Rosa has to cancel her appointment.

2. ☐ **a.** Rosa is late for her appointment.
   ☐ **b.** The salon isn't very busy.
   ☐ **c.** Rosa will have to wait.

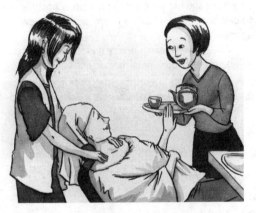

3. ☐ **a.** Rosa is leaving the salon.
   ☐ **b.** Rosa is getting a massage.
   ☐ **c.** Rosa doesn't want anything to drink.

4. ☐ **a.** Rosa didn't get a haircut.
   ☐ **b.** Rosa is pleased with her haircut.
   ☐ **c.** Rosa just got a pedicure.

12 **Write a short paragraph about Rosa's day at the salon.**

13 **WHAT ABOUT YOU? How do you like to pamper yourself?**

____ go to the hair salon   ____ go shopping

____ get a pedicure   ____ get a massage

____ get a shave and a haircut   ____ other: _____

LESSON 4

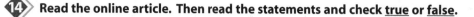

14 Read the online article. Then read the statements and check <u>true</u> or <u>false</u>.

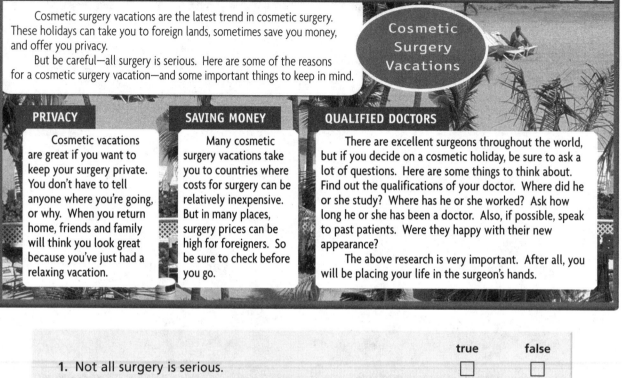

→ Cosmetic Surgery Vacations

Cosmetic surgery vacations are the latest trend in cosmetic surgery. These holidays can take you to foreign lands, sometimes save you money, and offer you privacy.

But be careful—all surgery is serious. Here are some of the reasons for a cosmetic surgery vacation—and some important things to keep in mind.

Cosmetic Surgery Vacations

PRIVACY

Cosmetic vacations are great if you want to keep your surgery private. You don't have to tell anyone where you're going, or why. When you return home, friends and family will think you look great because you've just had a relaxing vacation.

SAVING MONEY

Many cosmetic surgery vacations take you to countries where costs for surgery can be relatively inexpensive. But in many places, surgery prices can be high for foreigners. So be sure to check before you go.

QUALIFIED DOCTORS

There are excellent surgeons throughout the world, but if you decide on a cosmetic holiday, be sure to ask a lot of questions. Here are some things to think about. Find out the qualifications of your doctor. Where did he or she study? Where has he or she worked? Ask how long he or she has been a doctor. Also, if possible, speak to past patients. Were they happy with their new appearance?

The above research is very important. After all, you will be placing your life in the surgeon's hands.

	true	false
1. Not all surgery is serious.	☐	☐
2. Cosmetic surgery vacations don't always save you money.	☐	☐
3. You should always do research on the doctor.	☐	☐
4. It is hard to find good surgeons around the world.	☐	☐

15 CHALLENGE. Now answer the questions, according to the article.

1. What are the reasons to choose a cosmetic surgery vacation?

_____

2. What are some things that are important in a doctor?

_____

3. Why do you think some people prefer not to tell anyone when they get cosmetic surgery?

_____

_____

16 WHAT ABOUT YOU? Have you ever taken, or would you ever take, a cosmetic surgery vacation? Why or why not?

GRAMMAR BOOSTER

A Look in the medicine cabinet. Write sentences, using words from the box.

tube	bottle	container	package	bar

1. _There are four bottles of nail polish_ .

2. _____ .

3. _____ .

4. _____ .

5. _____ .

6. _____ .

B Check the correct sentences.

1. ☐ **a.** There isn't enough soap.

   ☐ **b.** There isn't too many soap.

2. ☐ **a.** Do you have too much razors?

   ☐ **b.** Do you have too many razors?

3. ☐ **a.** I don't have too many makeup.

   ☐ **b.** I don't have enough makeup.

4. ☐ **a.** Does she have too many toothpaste?

   ☐ **b.** Does she have enough toothpaste?

5. ☐ **a.** There isn't too much shampoo.

   ☐ **b.** There isn't too many shampoo.

C Complete each sentence with <u>too much</u>, <u>too many</u>, or <u>enough</u>.

1. I couldn't wash my hair. There wasn't _____ shampoo left.

2. I'm going to the store. Do you have _____ flour to make the cake?

3. There are just _____ people here. I don't feel like waiting.

4. Don't you think that's _____ money for a pedicure? It's too expensive!

5. You bought _____ nail files. We only need one.

D Complete each sentence with <u>something</u> or <u>anything</u>.

1. We have _____ new at our salon.

2. He didn't take _____ for his headache.

3. Do you need _____ from the drugstore?

4. I didn't see _____ I like in the catalog.

5. I always buy _____ from that store.

6. I just can't relax. There is always _____ to do.

7. They gave me _____ to drink at the salon.

8. I don't know _____ about cosmetic surgery.

E Read the paragraph. Find five mistakes and correct them.

I went to the supermarket today because I needed to get nothing to cook

for my dinner party tonight. I wanted to buy some juice, too. But when I got

there, there wasn't nothing on the shelf! I went to the store manager and

told him that the shelves were empty. He apologized and said there was

anything wrong with the delivery truck. "It didn't come today," he told me.

He said I'd have to wait until the next day. Now I don't have something to

serve for the big party tonight. I've never seen nothing like this!

JUST FOR FUN

1 WORD FIND. **Find 15 personal care products in the puzzle. The words are across (→), down (↓), diagonal (↘), and sometimes backwards (←). Circle the items.**

R	A	Z	O	R	B	L	A	D	E	N	L	N	D	U
R	E	T	E	M	O	M	R	E	H	T	S	O	E	S
J	E	A	S	U	P	O	J	A	Q	H	T	I	O	T
F	G	P	T	U	Z	U	I	M	A	Z	H	T	D	Y
Q	F	B	P	A	N	R	E	V	J	S	V	O	O	Q
Y	L	S	R	I	S	S	I	K	U	T	P	L	R	T
Z	L	C	V	P	L	N	C	R	A	J	S	Y	A	H
E	Y	J	R	B	G	C	B	R	J	M	Z	D	N	S
O	V	A	H	C	S	H	L	T	E	W	G	O	T	U
C	Y	I	R	I	T	O	L	I	G	E	X	B	U	R
T	O	E	C	O	M	B	A	O	A	G	N	H	L	B
P	A	D	O	V	M	Y	A	P	U	N	C	W	J	R
M	P	T	W	W	Q	N	B	S	E	B	K	F	I	V
O	T	B	X	A	R	A	C	S	A	M	T	X	Q	F
A	W	R	U	S	Z	A	S	B	U	I	C	H	A	H

body lotion
brush
comb
deodorant
hair spray
makeup
mascara
nail clipper
razor
razor blade
shaving cream
soap
sunscreen
thermometer
toothbrush

SOURCE: Created by Puzzlemaker at DiscoverySchool.com

2 TAKE A GUESS! **Read these sentences about hair. Do you think they are true or false? Write T (true) or F (false) and then check your answers.**

1. ___ Hair grows about 12 millimeters per month and one hair lives for up to seven years.

2. ___ If you never cut your hair, it would grow to a length of 107 centimeters before falling out.

3. ___ There are 120,000 hairs on the average adult head.

4. ___ Hair grows faster in the summer, during sleep, and between the ages of 16 and 24.

5. ___ Between the ages of 40 and 50, women lose about 20 percent of their hair.

SOURCE: www.ukhairdressers.com

(BEFORE) (AFTER)

Dr. M. J. Pilkington
COSMETIC SURGEON
CALL 1-800-NEWFACE

Eating Well

TOPIC PREVIEW

1 Look at the food pyramid. Write **T** (true), **F** (false), or **NI** (no information).

1. The healthiest foods are at the top of the pyramid. ____

2. You should avoid vegetable oils at most meals. ____

3. Whole-grain bread is healthier than white bread. ____

4. Pasta is healthier than fruit. ____

5. You should eat more seafood than poultry. ____

6. Exercise is an important part of a healthy life. ____

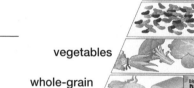

red meat, butter

sweets, pasta, potatoes, white rice, white bread

dairy

seafood, eggs, poultry

nuts and legumes

vegetables

fruits

whole-grain foods

vegetable oils

daily exercise and weight control

2 Choose the correct response. Circle the letter.

1. "Want to try some of the chocolate cookies?"

   a. No, thanks. I'm on a diet.   b. I used to. Not anymore.

2. "Why did you stop going to the gym?"

   a. Well, I would.   b. It was just too much trouble.

3. "Don't you usually drive to work?"

   a. Don't tell anyone.   b. I used to. Not anymore.

4. "What in the world are you doing?"

   a. Renting a car online.   b. I don't believe it.

5. "Aren't you on a diet?"

   a. Yes, you only live once!   b. Yes, I am.

3 WHAT ABOUT YOU? Do you think you have healthy or unhealthy eating habits? What kinds of food do you eat? Use your own words.

LESSON 1

4 ► Choose the correct response. Write the letter on the line.

1. _____ "Please help yourself."

2. _____ "I'll pass on the chocolates."

3. _____ "I'm sorry. I didn't know you were on a diet."

4. _____ "Why don't we go for a walk after dinner?"

a. Good idea. Let's go!

b. Thanks. Everything smells so good.

c. Don't worry about it.

d. Don't you eat sweets?

5 ► Complete the conversation. Use phrases from the box. Use each only once.

| is a vegetarian   is on a diet   is allergic to   doesn't care for   is avoiding |

A: Let's have a dinner party Friday night. Help me prepare the menu.

B: OK. Remember that my sister _____,
1.

so we can't make anything too fatty. Why don't you make some chicken?

A: I would, but Stella _____.
2.

She never eats meat. Maybe I can make that rice dish.

B: I don't know. Miguel is trying to eat healthy,

whole-grain foods, so he _____ white rice these days.
3.

A: OK. . . . Then how about black bean soup with peppers?

B: Uh, I don't think Julio would like that. He _____ spicy food.
4.

A: Is there anything that everyone can eat?

B: Hmm . . . I don't know, but I hope you'll make that delicious chocolate cake for dessert!

A: I can't. Don't you remember how sick Paul was at our last dinner?

He _____ chocolate!
5.

B: Why don't we just go out to eat?

A: Good idea!

6 ► WHAT ABOUT YOU? Fill in the blanks with a food item to make the sentences true for you.

1. I eat too much / many _____.

2. I'm avoiding _____.

3. I don't care for _____.

4. I really like to eat _____.

5. _____ doesn't / don't agree with me.

7 Complete each negative __yes__ / __no__ question.

1. **A:** _Didn't you go to Latvia_ _____ last year?

   B: Yes, I did. I went to Latvia in August.

2. **A:** _____ meat?

   B: No, I don't. I never touch meat.

3. **A:** _____ a doctor?

   B: No, she's not. David's mother is a dentist.

4. **A:** _____ a wonderful play?

   B: Yes, it was terrific.

5. **A:** _____ some more noodles?

   B: No, thanks. I'm full. I've had enough.

6. **A:** _____ China before?

   B: Actually, no. I've been to Japan.

LESSON 2

8 Choose the correct response. Circle the letter.

1. "Have you tried the steak? It's delicious!"

   a. No, thanks. I'm a big meat eater.　　**b.** No, thanks. I can't stand steak.　　**c.** I used to, but now I'm a vegetarian.

2. "Are you a big coffee drinker?"

   a. The coffee's terrific!　　**b.** It's not a problem.　　**c.** Actually, I've been cutting back.

3. "I'm crazy about chocolate. What about you?"

   a. I'm a big chocolate eater.　　**b.** Yes, thank you.　　**c.** I don't care for coffee.

9 What do you think they are saying? Write sentences about these people and their food passions. Use the words and phrases from the box. Use each only once.

~~crazy about~~　　don't care for　　big ___ eater　　love　　addict　　can't stand

1. _I'm crazy about asparagus._ _____

2. _____

3. _____

4. _____
_____
_____

5. _____
_____
_____

6. _____
_____
_____

10 Read about Kate's food passions. Then complete each sentence with <u>used to</u> or <u>didn't use to</u> and the verb.

When I was a kid, I loved sweets. I think I ate about five cookies a day! When I was a teenager, I started eating a lot of meat. I had steaks and fries almost every day. I didn't care for vegetables or fruit. Then on my 20th birthday, I decided I needed a change, so I became a vegetarian. These days I eat meat again, but I avoid fatty foods and sugar. I've lost a lot of weight and I feel much better.

1. Kate _____ a lot of sweets, but now she avoids sugar.
   (eat)

2. When she was a teenager, she _____ fatty foods.
   (have)

3. Before she turned 20, she _____ vegetables.
   (like)

4. She _____ a vegetarian, but now she eats meat.
   (be)

5. Kate _____ care of herself, but now she eats well.
   (take)

11 WHAT ABOUT YOU? Talk about your food passions and eating habits. Complete the paragraph. Use your <u>own</u> words.

I used to eat a lot of

LESSON 3

12 Read the online article about healthy lifestyle changes. Then write <u>T</u> (true) or <u>F</u> (false) for each statement below, according to the article.

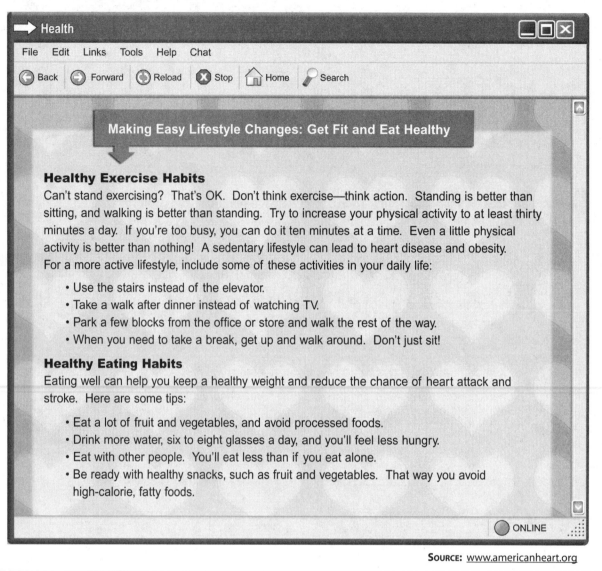

Source: www.americanheart.org

_____ 1. Using the stairs doesn't count as exercise, so you should use the elevator whenever you can. It doesn't make any difference to your health anyway.

_____ 2. Snacks such as grapes and carrots that are low in calories are better than potato chips or chocolates.

_____ 3. When you eat by yourself, you'll probably eat less because it's boring when there's no one to enjoy and share the food with.

_____ 4. The chance of heart attack and stroke is the same for people who are fit and lead an active lifestyle and for people who are obese and lead a sedentary lifestyle.

_____ 5. The worst thing to do when you need a break is to get up and walk around. You only get more tired that way. You should sit down and relax.

_____ 6. Drinking a lot of water reduces the feeling of hunger, so you may end up eating less.

13 CHALLENGE. **Read the letter and then finish the advice column. Use your <u>own</u> words and ideas.**

Dear Health Advisor:

I recently moved to a new city and got a new job. I have to sit at my desk all day, and then I sit at home and watch TV all evening. In the last four months, I have gained twenty pounds! I can't stand being overweight. What should I do?

Frank

Dear Frank:

It sounds like you have made some negative lifestyle changes. Here are three easy, positive lifestyle changes you can start making today:

1. _____ .

2. _____ .

3. _____ .

You'll feel much better!

LESSON 4

14 **Read the postcard. Fill in the blanks with the correct form of <u>taste</u>, <u>smell</u>, or <u>look</u>.**

Hi Reiko,

I'm having a great time in Marrakech! Yesterday I walked in the main square, and it _____ like a scene from a movie!
1.
People in long, beautiful robes were everywhere, and there was so much food! I saw some fish that _____ like the kind we have
2.
at home. Somewhere else in the market, I couldn't see where, there was a kind of grilled meat that _____ terrific. I found it, but didn't know if I should try it.
3.
It _____ kind of strange, but I bought some anyway. It was delicious!
4.
It _____ both spicy and sweet. It wasn't at all what I expected!
5.
You should come here on your next vacation!

See you soon,

Junko

15 List some foods that go with the descriptions.

1. spicy _____

2. crunchy _____

3. sweet _____

4. sour _____

5. hard _____

6. chewy _____

7. salty _____

16 WHAT ABOUT YOU? Complete the paragraph. Describe an unusual food you have eaten. Where and when did you eat it? What did it look, smell, and taste like? Would you recommend it to someone or not?

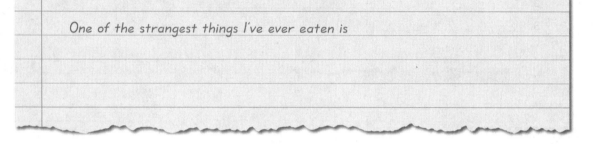

One of the strangest things I've ever eaten is

GRAMMAR BOOSTER

A Fill in the blanks to make negative yes / no questions. Then use the information in parentheses to answer the questions with a short answer.

1. A: _____ you have a vegetarian friend?
   B: _____.
   (None of my friends are vegetarian.)

2. A: _____ you trying to lose weight?
   B: _____.
   (I'm on a diet.)

3. A: _____ he like spicy food?
   B: _____.
   (He hates spicy food.)

4. A: _____ there sardines on that pizza?
   B: _____.
   (The pizza has sardines on it.)

5. A: _____ Sandra allergic to fish?
   B: _____.
   (She doesn't have any problem eating fish.)

B Complete each conversation with a suggestion, using Why don't or Why doesn't.

1. A: I'm too tired to cook dinner tonight.
   B: _Why don't we_____ go out to eat?

2. A: Fred's old van keeps breaking down.
   B: _____ buy a new car?

3. A: My mother thinks the hotel room will be too small.
   B: _____ reserve a suite?

4. A: That film was really long and boring!
   B: _____ watch a short comedy next time?

C ▷ Read the statement and then answer the question, using an appropriate form of <u>used to</u> for each of the following.

1. "Since Charlie started going to the gym every day, he's lost so much weight."

   Did Charlie use to go to the gym every day?

   No, he didn't use to go to the gym every day .

2. "Now that he has more time, Scott has started making dinner every night."

   Did Scott use to make dinner every night?

   _____ .

3. "Paul began getting up early every day when he had children."

   Did Paul use to get up early every day before he had children?

   _____ .

4. "As Cindy got older, her tastes changed, and now she actually likes eating vegetables."

   Did Cindy use to like eating vegetables?

   _____ .

5. "I can't believe Judy has become a vegetarian!"

   Did Judy use to eat meat?

   _____ .

6. "When Peter's doctor told him that he had better stop smoking, he quit."

   Did Peter use to smoke?

   _____ .

7. "Soon after Pamela and Ed got married, they bought their first house."

   Did Pamela and Ed use to have a house before they got married?

   _____ .

D ▷ Write a <u>yes</u> / <u>no</u> question for each response, using a form of <u>used to</u>.

1. **A:** *Did you use to work in that part of the city* ?

   B: Yes, I did. I used to work in that part of the city a few years ago.

2. **A:** _____ ?

   B: No, they didn't. People didn't use to watch DVDs for entertainment.

3. **A:** _____ ?

   B: Yes, it did. Eating used to be simpler.

4. **A:** _____ ?

   B: No, they didn't. Foods didn't use to have labels.

5. **A:** _____ ?

   B: Yes, I did. I used to live closer to work.

6. **A:** _____ ?

   B: Yes, they did. Cars used to use a lot more gas.

1 ▶ **Read the clues and complete the crossword puzzle.**

Across

4. It's a long, green (or white) vegetable.

6. They are white and yellow inside, and they come from a chicken.

8. It's raw fish on rice.

9. They're made from cocoa beans. People often give them in a box as a gift.

Down

1. It's made of milk, it's sweet, and it comes in many flavors.

2. It's made with soybeans and is popular in Asia and with vegetarians all over the world.

3. These are small fish that are usually very salty.

5. This is a little like fish but comes in a shell. Some people are allergic to this.

7. Vegetarians never eat this.

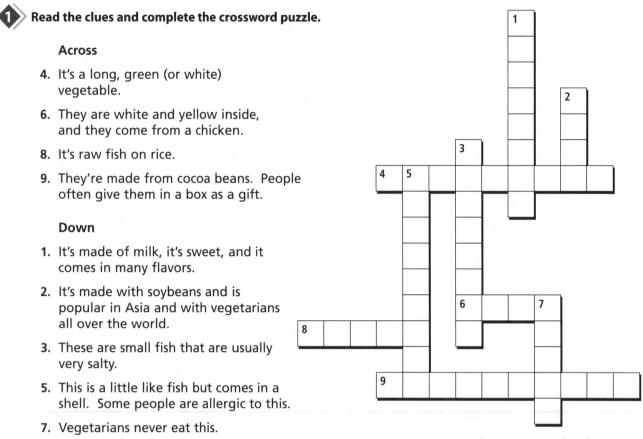

SOURCE: www.puzzlemaker.com

2 ▶ BRAINTEASER. **Look at the picture and then read the clues. Write the name on the line.**

2. _____

4. _____

1. _____

3. _____

5. _____

Clues:

- Patty doesn't care for vegetables.
- Al's allergic to dairy products.
- Fish doesn't agree with Greg.
- Marcia is a vegetarian.
- Nicolas is trying to lose weight.

Psychology and Personality

TOPIC PREVIEW

1 Look at the color tests and the pictures of the two women. Based on the answers to the tests and the results, who do you think is Michelle and who do you think is Janet? Label the pictures.

COLOR TEST   Name: **Michelle Duval**

1) Which color do you prefer for shoes?
   - ☑ black   ○ white
   - ○ light brown   ○ red

2) Which color of clothes do you prefer to wear?
   - ○ green   ☑ gray
   - ○ white   ○ pink

3) Which color makes you feel sad?
   - ○ white   ○ dark blue
   - ○ silver   ☑ orange

4) What color would you paint your bedroom?
   - ○ gold   ○ purple
   - ☑ dark gray   ○ green

5) Which color do you think is the most relaxing?
   - ☑ purple   ○ yellow
   - ○ green   ○ blue

RESULT

According to your answers, you probably keep your feelings inside most of the time. You often feel sad and down.

1. _____

2. _____

COLOR TEST   Name: **Janet Gamble**

1) Which color do you prefer for shoes?
   - ○ black   ○ white
   - ○ light brown   ☑ red

2) Which color of clothes do you prefer to wear?
   - ○ green   ○ gray
   - ○ white   ☑ pink

3) Which color makes you feel sad?
   - ○ white   ☑ dark blue
   - ○ silver   ○ orange

4) What color would you paint your bedroom?
   - ☑ gold   ○ purple
   - ○ dark gray   ○ green

5) Which color do you think is the most relaxing?
   - ○ purple   ☑ yellow
   - ○ green   ○ blue

RESULT

According to your answers, you probably don't have any problems expressing your feelings. You are always cheerful and happy.

2 WHAT ABOUT YOU? Fill in the chart. Which color makes you feel . . .

happy? _____

lucky? _____

calm? _____

powerful? _____

down in the dumps? _____

FACTOID: Men, women, and colors

Studies have found that women prefer red over blue, but men prefer blue over red.

SOURCE: www.colormatters.com

3 Choose the sentence that has a similar meaning. Circle the letter.

1. I just feel a little out of sorts.

   a. I am just kind of busy.   **b.** I don't feel quite right.

2. Nothing I can put my finger on.

   a. It's not anything exactly.   **b.** I don't need anything to eat.

3. Michael's been feeling a bit blue lately.

   a. Michael's been a little sad lately.   **b.** Michael's been feeling quite great lately.

4. Maybe a good comedy would cheer you up.

   a. Maybe you shouldn't see a good comedy.   **b.** Maybe a good comedy would make you feel better.

LESSON 1

4 Put the conversation in order. Write the number on the line.

_1_ Dad, can I paint my bedroom?

___ It's depressing.

___ How about red or black?

___ Why? What's wrong with black?

___ Well, red's OK, but black is out of the question.

___ Sure. What color?

_7_ To me, black is calm, not depressing.

> **FACTOID: Olympic Colors**
>
> The official Olympic logo was created by Baron Pierre de Coubertin in 1913. It consists of five interlacing rings of blue, yellow, black, green, and red. At least one of these colors is found in the flag of every nation.

SOURCE: www.colormatters.com

5 CHALLENGE. Complete Lucia's letter. Use gerunds and infinitives. Remember to put the verbs in the correct tense.

Hi Rebecca:

   Well, I finally made a change! Last week I said to myself, "I _____ at our old
                                                                1. can't stand / look

kitchen walls one more day!" So I _____ them! My roommate Sara said we
                                        2. decide / repaint

should _____ a plan before we do it. She even _____
        3. discuss / make   **4. suggest / take**

a month or two to think about it. She said we should _____ first, but I already
                                                        5. practice / paint

know how to paint. I don't _____. Anyway, I _____ new things.
                            6. need / learn   **7. not mind / try**

Finally, we _____ the kitchen a cheerful color—bright yellow! I'm not sure, but
            8. choose / give

Sara _____ the new color. In fact, I don't think she _____!
      9. not seem / like   **10. enjoy / paint**

But I hope she does, because I _____ the living room next. I _____
                              11. plan / paint   **12. would like / paint**

it fuchsia! What do you think about that?

Lucia

6 Complete each sentence with a word from the box. Use each word only once.

| depressing | calm | exciting | cheerful | disgusting | nervous |

1. I hate this theater. The lobby always smells terrible, and the bathrooms are dirty and

   _____.

2. Don't get _____ when you hear the fire alarm. Be sure to stay _____.

3. Last night's ball game was so _____! Our team won the championship!

4. Penny is such a(n) _____ person. She always gives you a big smile when she

   sees you.

5. I don't feel like watching that film. I hear it's very _____. I'm not in the mood

   for a sad movie.

LESSON 2

7 Complete the conversation. Use the correct preposition with the verb or adjective, and a gerund.

A: You look a little blue. What's up?

B: Oh, nothing really. I'm just _tired of working_____ late every night.
   1. tired / work

A: Is that all? You really look down.

B: I'm _____ the same thing every day. And I also feel
   2. bored / do

   _____ too little time at home.
   3. sad / spend

A: Have you _____ overtime?
   4. complained / work

B: No. I'm _____ my boss angry. I had to _____ a
   5. afraid / make   **6. apologize / finish**

   report late. And now my boss is _____ us more work.
   7. talking / give

A: Wow! I see why you are feeling blue. Why don't you start looking for a new job?

8 Suggest something to cheer these people up. Write complete sentences.

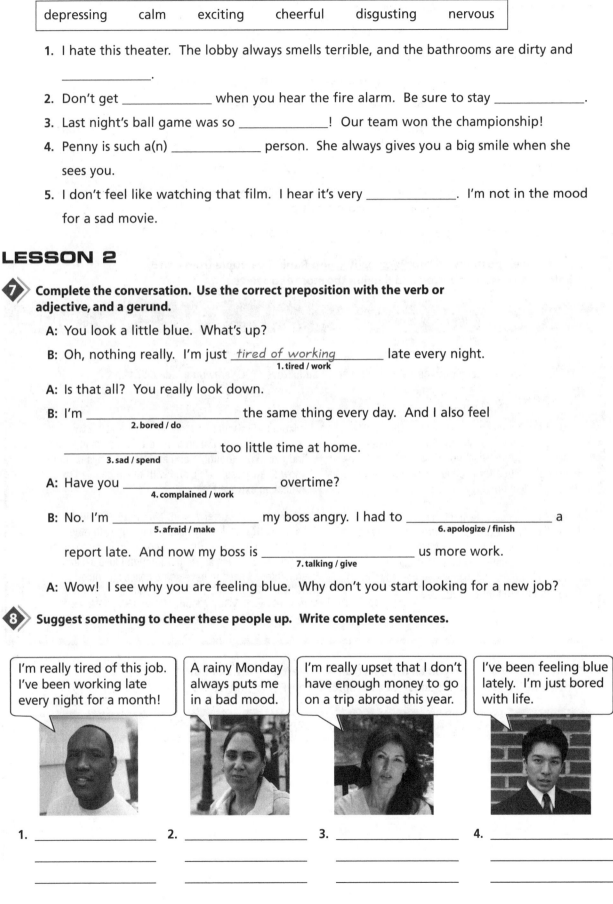

I'm really tired of this job. I've been working late every night for a month!

A rainy Monday always puts me in a bad mood.

I'm really upset that I don't have enough money to go on a trip abroad this year.

I've been feeling blue lately. I'm just bored with life.

1. _____   2. _____   3. _____   4. _____

_____   _____   _____   _____

_____   _____   _____   _____

LESSON 3

9 ▸ **Complete each sentence. Circle the letter.**

1. He's got a great ____. I just love spending time with him!

   a. personality   **b.** nurture   **c.** genetics

2. When I need to think, I prefer to be alone with my ____.

   a. genetics   **b.** nature   **c.** thoughts

3. Some people believe that your personality comes from your ____, that is, your friends, your experiences, and everything around you.

   a. nature   **b.** thoughts   **c.** environment

4. I believe personality has nothing to do with one's home or friends, but more to do with ____ —traits that come from one's parents.

   a. emotions   **b.** genetics   **c.** thoughts

10 ▸ **Read the web postings on <u>YourPersonality.com</u>. Rank the people from 1 to 5, 1 being the most introverted and 5 being the most extroverted.**

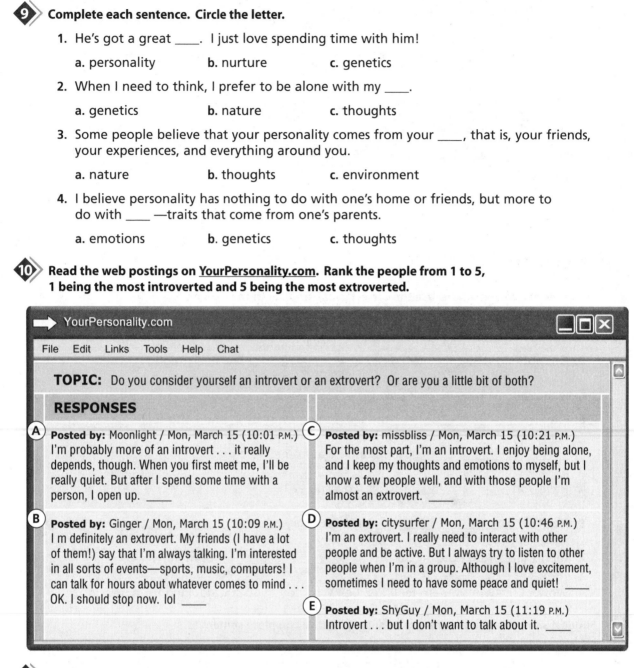

YourPersonality.com   ▭◻✕

File   Edit   Links   Tools   Help   Chat

TOPIC: Do you consider yourself an introvert or an extrovert? Or are you a little bit of both?

RESPONSES

(A) **Posted by:** Moonlight / Mon, March 15 (10:01 P.M.)
I'm probably more of an introvert . . . it really depends, though. When you first meet me, I'll be really quiet. But after I spend some time with a person, I open up. ____

(B) **Posted by:** Ginger / Mon, March 15 (10:09 P.M.)
I m definitely an extrovert. My friends (I have a lot of them!) say that I'm always talking. I'm interested in all sorts of events—sports, music, computers! I can talk for hours about whatever comes to mind . . . OK. I should stop now. lol ____

(C) **Posted by:** missbliss / Mon, March 15 (10:21 P.M.)
For the most part, I'm an introvert. I enjoy being alone, and I keep my thoughts and emotions to myself, but I know a few people well, and with those people I'm almost an extrovert. ____

(D) **Posted by:** citysurfer / Mon, March 15 (10:46 P.M.)
I'm an extrovert. I really need to interact with other people and be active. But I always try to listen to other people when I'm in a group. Although I love excitement, sometimes I need to have some peace and quiet! ____

(E) **Posted by:** ShyGuy / Mon, March 15 (11:19 P.M.)
Introvert . . . but I don't want to talk about it. ____

11 ▸ **WHAT ABOUT YOU? Are you an introvert, an extrovert, or a little of both? Write a web posting in response to the topic on <u>YourPersonality.com</u>.**

YourPersonality.com   ▭◻✕

File   Edit   Links   Tools   Help   Chat

Posted by: _____

_____

_____

_____

_____

Read the article and answer the questions below.

ASTROLOGY — FINDING YOUR PERSONALITY IN THE STARS

Why do you think and act the way you do? What is the secret to your thoughts and emotions? Why do you have the personality you do? Is it nature or nurture? Genetics or the environment? Or could it be the sun and the stars?

Some people think that birth order influences personality, but many others believe that the day you were born on influences your personality. These people believe in astrology. They believe that the sun and the stars influence human personality and events.

Astrology may be a way to understand human personality. Or it may be a false science. But millions of people around the world read their astrological horoscope every day—just in case!

 Aquarius ≈≈≈
Jan 20–Feb 18
- very active
- cheerful
- can be a clown

 **Gemini** Ⅱ
May 21–Jun 21
- worries about things
- can be self-critical
- can be hard to know

 **Libra** ♎
Sept 23–Oct 23
- conservative
- spends time with a few friends
- has strong emotions

 **Pisces** ♓
Feb 19–Mar 20
- honest
- easily bored with jobs
- likes quiet time

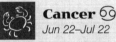 **Cancer** ♋
Jun 22–Jul 22
- interested in travel
- enjoys being with other people
- always behaves appropriately

 Scorpio ♏
Oct 24–Nov 21
- friendly
- sensitive to others' emotions
- not easy to get to know

 **Aries** ♈
Mar 21–Apr 19
- enjoys being alone
- hard to get to know
- keeps thoughts and emotions inside

 Leo ♌
Jul 23–Aug 22
- happy with lots of people
- cheers people up
- crazy about nature

 Sagittarius ♐
Nov 22–Dec 21
- creative
- likes everything in moderation
- gets along with everyone

 **Taurus** ♉
Apr 20–May 20
- calm
- seeks peace
- good listener

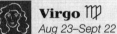 **Virgo** ♍
Aug 23–Sept 22
- keeps ideas inside
- likes to spend time alone
- enjoys reading

 **Capricorn** ♑
Dec 22–Jan 19
- has a lot of friends
- interested in events
- loves excitement

1. What is the basic idea behind astrology? _____

_____.

2. Which of the zodiac signs describe more of an introvert? _____.

3. Which signs describe more of an extrovert? _____.

4. What sign of the zodiac are you? _____ Does the description for your sign

describe you? Why or why not? _____

_____.

GRAMMAR BOOSTER

A Complete each sentence. Circle the letter.

1. I love ____ TV in the evening.
   a. watch   **b.** to watch   **c.** watched

2. I hurt my knee last month, so I quit ____.
   a. jog   **b.** to jog   **c.** jogging

3. ____ too many sweets is bad for you.
   a. Eating   **b.** Eat   **c.** Eaten

4. My favorite thing to do after work is ____ magazines.
   a. read   **b.** to reading   **c.** to read

5. If you get an early start, you'll have a better chance of ____ your work on time.
   a. finish   **b.** finishing   **c.** to finish

6. Do you mind my ____ the window? It's freezing in here!
   a. closing   **b.** close   **c.** closed

7. ____ opera well is a hard thing to do.
   a. Sing   **b.** To sing   **c.** To singing

B Complete each sentence with a gerund or an infinitive. Use verbs from the box.
Use each verb only once.

| cook   play   study   do   watch   ride |

1. Susan can't stand _____ the dishes after dinner.

2. Michael loves _____ the guitar.

3. Marianna hates _____ for exams.

4. Joseph would like _____ his bike.

5. Beth doesn't mind _____ for her family.

6. Jim likes _____ TV.

C Find and correct six errors in the diary.

> Usually I don't mind studying, but last night I was so sick of do homework that I decided
> to go out with Amy. She felt like go to the movies, so I suggested to go to a romantic comedy.
> But Amy said she hates romantic movies and suggested watch an action movie instead. But I
> can't stand so much violence, so finally we chose seeing that new Japanese animated film.
> We both really enjoyed to watch it, and we had a wonderful time.

D Unscramble the words and phrases to complete the conversations. Use a gerund or an infinitive.

1. **A:** _John can't stand thinking about graduation_____.
   think / John / about / can't stand / graduation

   B: I know. _____.
   He / leave / hates / his friends

2. **A:** _____.
   refuse / dinner / tonight / I / make

   B: Fine by me. _____.
   don't mind / go / I / out to eat

3. **A:** _____?
   buy / discussed / Have / you and Peter / a house

   B: Yes. _____.
   find / We / would like / something bigger

4. **A:** _____.
   tonight / you / I / see / didn't expect

   B: Well, _____.
   at the last minute / I / decided / come

E Complete each sentence with an affirmative or negative gerund.

1. You should start _____ every day if you want to lose weight.
   exercise

2. Sue was worried about _____ enough money to pay her bills.
   have

3. When will you finish _____ on that project?
   work

4. Avoid _____ a cell phone while you're driving.
   use

5. Stella and I have considered _____ a new car. We just don't have the money.
   buy

6. I apologize for _____ you that I'd be late. I'm sorry that you've waited so long.
   tell

7. Jeff really dislikes _____ to strangers. He's such an introvert!
   talk

8. A good way to learn English is to practice _____ a diary in English.
   write

9. I believe in _____ fatty foods. You'll be healthier.
   eat

JUST FOR FUN

1 Unscramble the letters to form words.

1. (TTROERVEX)   E X __ __ __ __ __ __ __

2. (SONTYERPALI)   P __ __ __ __ __ __ __ __ __ __

3. (TURUREN)   N __ __ __ __ __

4. (NOTIOEM)   E __ __ __ __ __ __

5. (MRAGINHC)   C H __ __ __ __ __ __

6. (BIILSNG)   S __ __ __ __ __ __

2 Choose the best word from the box to describe each person. Write the word under the picture.

creative	self-critical	rebel	introvert	clown	conservative

1. _____

2. _____

3. _____

4. _____

5. _____

6. _____

3 FIGURE IT OUT! Here are the names of four colors with the vowels removed. What are the four colors?

PLTNM   MV   FCHS   CRM

Enjoying the Arts

TOPIC PREVIEW

 Look at the two paintings and read the conversation.

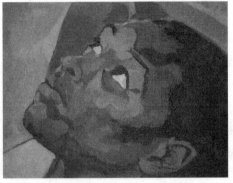

Serena by Jessica Miller-Smith, U.S.A (2000)

Thoughts by Agnes Geniusaite, Lithuania (1997)

Gerald: This painting is really weird. Is that by Jessica Miller-Smith?

Sophie: Yes. It says it was painted in 2000.

Gerald: I don't like it. It makes me feel nervous. What do you think?

Sophie: I think it's pretty cool. I find it exciting. It would look fantastic in my bedroom.

Gerald: Ugh! I'd rather look at a plain wall.

Gerald: Hey, look at this incredible painting! It says it's by Agnes Geniusaite. I'm just crazy about her stuff.

Sophie: I think it's sort of depressing.

Gerald: Really? Maybe you're just feeling a little blue today.

Sophie: Maybe. But I don't care for it at all. I'm not that crazy about dark colors.

Gerald: Well, to each his own.

Now check the statements that are true.

☐ **1.** Gerald thinks Jessica Miller-Smith is pretty cool.

☐ **2.** Sophie likes Miller-Smith.

☐ **3.** Gerald likes Agnes Geniusaite's art.

☐ **4.** Sophie finds Geniusaite's painting depressing.

☐ **5.** Sophie prefers darker colors to brighter colors.

☐ **6.** Sophie and Gerald like the same kind of art.

2 **Write a plus (+) next to the statements that indicate that the person likes the art, and a minus (−) next to the statements that indicate that the person doesn't like it.**

____ **1.** I'd rather look at a plain wall.

____ **2.** Her photographs are wonderful.

____ **3.** It's an unforgettable film.

____ **4.** Don't you think Vera Wang's fashions are gorgeous?

____ **5.** Actually, I find them kind of boring.

____ **6.** To tell you the truth, I'm not too crazy about it.

____ **7.** Oh, I'm really into it!

____ **8.** I used to be into photography, but not now.

3 ▸ Choose the correct response. Circle the letter.

1. "We should buy this painting. It would look great in our living room!"

   a. What do you think?   b. I'd rather look at a plain wall.   c. I used to be into films.

2. "Don't you find this painting a little too dark?"

   a. Well, to each his own.   b. No. I like bright colors.   c. No. I think it's just right.

3. "I think Anne Klein's fashions are fantastic. What about you?"

   a. Is it a Picasso?   b. I find them boring.   c. They were painted in 1903.

4. "Just look at the colors in this photograph. Aren't they amazing?"

   a. This sculpture is sort of interesting.   b. Maybe you're just feeling blue today.   c. Honestly, I'm not crazy about really bright colors.

5. "That film is really weird. I don't think anyone cares for it at all."

   a. I kind of like it, actually.   b. Is it a drawing?   c. It would look nice over my desk.

4 ▸ WHAT ABOUT YOU? What do you think of the paintings in Exercise 1? Fill in the chart.

	Miller-Smith	Geniusaite
What do you like about it?		
What do you dislike about it?		
Where would you hang it?		

LESSON 1

5 ▸ Read a page from a tour guide about Paris. Make a recommendation to someone who is visiting Paris. Complete the conversation, using the information in the tour guide.

The Rodin Museum

There are many wonderful museums to see while you are visiting Paris. One museum you should be sure to visit is the lovely Rodin Museum. The Rodin Museum houses over 6,600 sculptures. There is also an impressive garden. A large number of sculptures are presented in this setting, including Rodin's most famous work, *The Thinker*. In addition to the sculptures, take a look at the excellent drawing collection. Many of Rodin's sketches are there.

YOU Be sure _____
1.
in Paris.

B: Really? Why's that?

YOU Well, _____.
2.

B: No kidding!

YOU They also _____.
3.

You'll _____.
4.

B: Thanks for the recommendation.

6 ▸ **Read each sentence and decide if it's in the active voice (A) or passive voice (P).**

1. Many people visit the Metropolitan Museum of Art in New York. ____

2. The glass pyramid in front of the Louvre was finished in 1989. ____

3. A color poster of the painting was made available. ____

4. The museum catalog has been translated into many languages. ____

5. Akira Kurosawa directed the film *Seven Samurai* in 1954. ____

6. That vase was made in ancient Egypt. ____

7. The photograph was taken fifty years ago. ____

8. Matisse painted *La Musique* in 1910. ____

7 ▸ **CHALLENGE. Use the information in the chart to write two sentences. Write the first sentence in the active voice and the second one in the passive voice. Be sure to use the correct verb with the artwork.**

Art Object	Artist	Year
1. *Still Life with Watermelon* (painting)	Pablo Picasso	1946
2. *Vines and Olive Trees* (painting)	Joan Miró	1919
3. *The Raven and the First Men* (wood figure)	Bill Reid	1994
4. *A. I.* (film)	Steven Spielberg	2002
5. *Waterfront Demonstration* (photograph)	Dorothea Lange	1934

1. Active: *Pablo Picasso painted "Still Life with Watermelon" in 1946* _____.

   Passive: *"Still Life with Watermelon" was painted by Pablo Picasso in 1946* _____.

2. Active: _____.

   Passive: _____.

3. Active: _____.

   Passive: _____.

4. Active: _____.

   Passive: _____.

5. Active: _____.

   Passive: _____.

LESSON 2

8 ▸ **Choose the correct response. Write the letter on the line.**

1. ____ "Is this vase handmade?"

2. ____ "What do you think of this painting?"

3. ____ "Where was the figure made?"

4. ____ "Do you know when this photograph was taken?"

5. ____ "What's the bowl made of?"

a. Clay. It's handmade.

b. Yes, it is.

c. It says it was made in Bulgaria.

d. Not much. I'm not too crazy about the colors.

e. Around 1980, I think.

9 Find a word in each row that describes each picture. Write sentences about the pictures, using the words. You will use some words more than once.

Material	cloth	glass	wood	stone	clay	gold
Object	bowl	figure	vase	bag		
Adjective	simple gorgeous	weird wonderful	beautiful boring	fantastic cheerful	lovely interesting	depressing cool

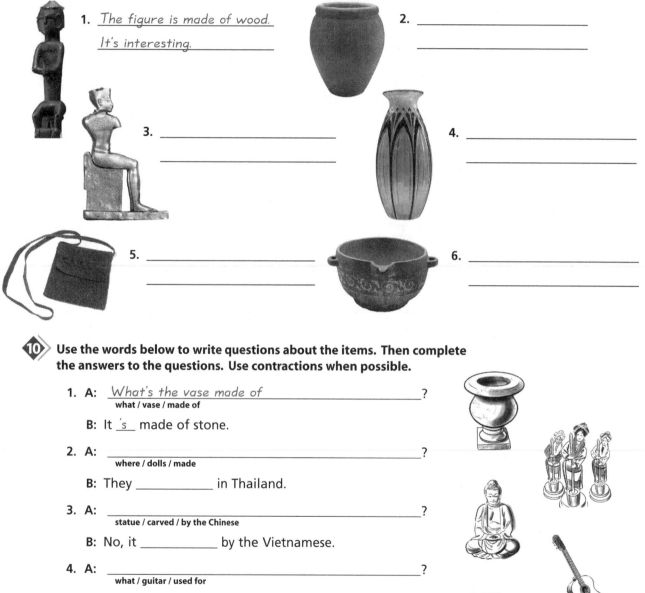

1. *The figure is made of wood. It's interesting.*

2. _____

3. _____

4. _____

5. _____

6. _____

10 Use the words below to write questions about the items. Then complete the answers to the questions. Use contractions when possible.

1. A: *What's the vase made of* _____?
   what / vase / made of

   B: It _'s_ made of stone.

2. A: _____?
   where / dolls / made

   B: They _____ in Thailand.

3. A: _____?
   statue / carved / by the Chinese

   B: No, it _____ by the Vietnamese.

4. A: _____?
   what / guitar / used for

   B: It _____ special festivals.

5. A: _____?
   how / chair / built

   B: It _____ by hand.

6. A: _____?
   robe / worn / in Japan

   B: Yes, _____ .

LESSON 3

 11 Read the advice column from *ArtNews*. Then rewrite each false statement as a true statement.

ArtNews — Ask Alice—Advice for New Artists

Dear Alice,

I saw my first Matisse painting when I was five years old. Since then, I have wanted to be a famous artist. I began studying art seriously five years ago and now I want to go to art school in Paris. Art is the one great love of my life. But my family doesn't know much about art. They have some art at home, of course, but they never go to museums. I go to museums almost every week. My family thinks I'm crazy. Am I?

Donald

Dear Donald,

It is wonderful that you are fascinated by art. But Paris is an expensive city and far away. Maybe you should go to an art school closer to your home. You will find it exciting to be around students who also love art. And who knows . . . maybe your family will become interested in art, too. Good luck!

Alice

1. Donald thinks his family is crazy. _____.

2. His family knows a lot about art. _____.

3. Donald saw his first Matisse painting five years ago. _____

_____.

4. He has been studying art since he was five years old. _____

_____.

5. Alice thinks Donald should go to art school in Paris. _____

_____.

 12 WHAT ABOUT YOU? Check the boxes that describe how Donald, his family, and <u>you</u> feel about art.

	Donald	His family	You
love(s) art	✔		
collect(s) art			
doesn't / don't care about art			
make(s) art			
want(s) to be an artist			
is / are crazy about art			
has / have artistic talent			
visit(s) art museums often			
has / have art at home			

13 WHAT ABOUT YOU? How does art fit into <u>your</u> life? Use the phrases in the chart in Exercise 12 to write a short paragraph about <u>yourself</u>.

LESSON 4

 14 Complete this biography of Pablo Picasso, using the passive voice.

Pablo Ruiz Picasso began studying art with his father. Then from 1895 until 1904, he painted in Barcelona. During this time, he made his first trip to Paris, where he _____
1. inspire
by the artwork of Henri de Toulouse-Lautrec.

In Paris, Picasso _____
2. influence
by all the poverty he saw. He was sad and angry that so many people lived without enough food or clothing. He painted many pictures of poor people to bring attention to their situation.

In 1906, Picasso met the artist Henri Matisse, who was to become his longtime friend. Picasso _____ in Matisse's style,
3. interest
but he did not imitate it. The artists he really admired were Georges Braque and Joan Miró. Picasso _____ by Braque's and
4. fascinate
Miró's work. Together the three artists started the movement known as Cubism.

One of Picasso's most famous artistic pieces is *Guernica*. Picasso _____ by the violence of
5. move
the Spanish Civil War. This prompted him to paint the piece.

15 CHALLENGE. Read the biography in Exercise 14 again. Rewrite the sentences, changing them from the passive voice to the active voice.

1. *The artwork of Henri de Toulouse-Lautrec inspired Picasso* _____.

2. _____.

3. _____.

4. _____.

5. _____.

16 WHAT ABOUT YOU? Write a paragraph about your favorite kind of art and your favorite artist. Use some of the phrases from the box.

| interested in | fascinated by | inspired by | moved by | influenced by |

I'm a big fan of _____. _____ *is my*

favorite _____.

GRAMMAR **BOOSTER**

A Complete each sentence. Circle the letter.

1. This vase _____ made in 1569.

   a. is   **b.** has   **c.** was   **d.** were

2. Coffee is _____ in Colombia.

   a. grow   **b.** grew   **c.** grown   **d.** been growing

3. Business cards _____ exchanged at the meeting.

   a. is   **b.** being   **c.** was   **d.** were

4. The art exhibition was _____ by over 1,000 people.

   a. attending   **b.** attended   **c.** attend   **d.** will attend

5. I _____ invited, but I went anyway.

   a. wasn't   **b.** hasn't   **c.** isn't   **d.** weren't

B Write sentences in the passive voice, using the verbs in parentheses.
Use the correct verb tenses.

1. French (speak) in Quebec, Canada. _____.

2. The Taj Mahal (build) around 1631. _____.

3. A new art museum (open) next year. _____.

4. These CDs (make) in Korea. _____.

5. "Let it Be" (write) by John Lennon. _____.

6. Your DVD player (repair) now. _____.

7. *Cornflowers* (paint) in 1876. _____.

8. The *Mona Lisa* (see) by millions of people since it was painted in the 16th century.

   _____.

C Read this description of a museum. Find and correct five mistakes in the use
of the passive voice. The first mistake is already corrected.

The Frick Collection

                           was built

The mansion of Henry Clay Frick ~~builded~~ in 1914 at the corner of Fifth Avenue and

East 70th Street in New York City. It later opened to the public. Several improvements

have made over the years. Works of Monet, El Greco, Bernini, Degas, Vermeer, and

many other artists found throughout the mansion. Some of the museum's large

collection of art is display at temporary exhibitions around the world.

D Rewrite the sentences in the passive voice. Use a <u>by</u> phrase only if it is important or necessary to know who or what is performing the action.

1. People in China made this DVD player.

   This DVD player was made in China _____.

2. Artists hand painted these plates in France.

   _____.

3. They make good cars in Japan and Korea.

   _____.

4. They sell Brazilian coffee all over the world.

   _____.

5. Swiss companies still make most of the world's best watches.

   _____.

6. Shakespeare wrote *King Lear*.

   _____.

E Rewrite the sentences in the passive voice in Exercise D as <u>yes</u> / <u>no</u> questions.

1. *Was this DVD player made in China* _____?

2. _____?

3. _____?

4. _____?

5. _____?

6. _____?

JUST FOR
FUN

1 Unscramble the letters to find what material each object is made of. Then match the item with the picture.

____ 1. r e l v i s _____ earrings

____ 2. y a l c _____ vase

____ 3. s a l g s _____ vase

____ 4. c h o t l _____ doll

____ 5. n e s t o _____ bowl

____ 6. d o o w _____ figure

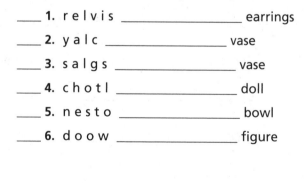

2 BRAINTEASER. **Who makes what? Read the clues and complete the sentences.**

1. The figure was sculpted by _____.

2. The photograph was taken by _____.

3. The suit was designed by _____.

4. The painting was done by _____.

5. The pottery was made by _____.

Clues:

Leo takes a lot of pictures.

Nicole works in the fashion industry.

Ju works with stone.

Brigitte's exhibit is at the gallery.

Jean uses clay in his work.

"Art washes away from the soul the dust of everyday life." – Pablo Picasso

Living with Computers

TOPIC PREVIEW

1 Read the four people's situations. What electronic items do you think they may need? Choose the items from the box and write them on the lines.

digital camera	cell phone	speaker	headset	PDA	CD drive
laptop	camcorder	printer	joystick	scanner	MP3 player

1. Tom is traveling to Europe. He wants to take a lot of pictures but doesn't want to bring a lot of film with him. He also wants to make a home video of his trip.

   _____ _____

   _____ _____

2. Mike is preparing for a speech for twenty people. He wants to give each person in the audience a copy of his five-page report. He also wants to add some photos to the report. His report is saved in his computer.

   _____ _____

   _____ _____

3. Gerry is very busy and has a lot of meetings in different cities every week. She needs to organize and remember all the things she needs to do. She also has to be able to send e-mails and make phone calls when she's on the road or out of town.

   _____ _____

   _____ _____

4. Shannon spends three hours on the bus every day. She wants to listen to music that she likes on the bus, but she doesn't want to have to carry a lot of CDs.

   _____ _____

   _____ _____

2 Choose the correct response. Circle the letter.

1. "Did you just log on?"
   a. No, thanks.　　　　b. Yes. What are you up to?　　　　c. I'm still here.

2. "Am I interrupting you?"
   a. Great!　　　　b. Sorry about that.　　　　c. Not at all.

3. "What are you up to?"
   a. Just deleting e-mail.　　　　b. Photos of my trip.　　　　c. They're awesome.

4. "Are you still there?"
   a. I just logged on.　　　　b. I'm still here.　　　　c. Sorry about that.

3 WHAT ABOUT YOU? Check the correct box to show how often these things happen in your life.

	Every day	Sometimes	Not very often	Never
I get e-mail.	☐	☐	☐	☐
I log on to the Internet.	☐	☐	☐	☐
My printer won't print.	☐	☐	☐	☐
I get instant messages.	☐	☐	☐	☐
My computer crashes.	☐	☐	☐	☐

LESSON 1

4. Look at the ads and complete the conversations with <u>as</u> ... <u>as</u> and the appropriate adjective.

1. **A:** I'm thinking of getting a new computer game system.

   B: Oh, yeah? What kind?

   A: I've heard Giga-Game is a lot of fun.

   B: Well, I think Game-Pro is just _as exciting as_ Giga-Game, but it's a lot cheaper.

   A: Really? So, Game-Pro isn't nearly _____ Giga-Game? I'll go check it out.

2. **A:** Did you get a new hard disk?

   B: Yeah, my XZ 5400 crashed, and I had to replace it with the YZ 2500.

   A: Are you satisfied with the new one? Is it very fast?

   B: Well, to tell the truth, it's not nearly _____ the old one!

3. **A:** Wow! Look at this! What do you think of the Monster Monitor? It's really big!

   B: Well, yeah, but the 40-40 monitor is just _____ the Monster.

4. **A:** I'm thinking of getting the C2000 digital camera. What do you think?

   B: I've heard the C2000 isn't quite _____ the Maxcam.

   A: Really? Are you sure? I thought they were the same price.

5 CHALLENGE. Look at the chart comparing two laptop computers. Complete the sentences, using **(not) as . . . as** and the adjective in parentheses. Use the adverbs **almost**, **quite**, **just**, and **nearly**.

	Laptop-To-Go	Laptop-Friend	KEY
Weight	.5 kilograms	1.5 kilograms	Better
Ease of use			
Monitor screen quality			
Software package			
Speed			
Cost	$999	$1,099	Worse

1. The quality of the Laptop-To-Go's monitor is *almost as good as* _____ the quality of the Laptop-Friend's monitor.
   <u>(good)</u>

2. Laptop-To-Go is _____ Laptop-Friend.
   <u>(expensive)</u>

3. Laptop-Friend is _____ Laptop-To-Go.
   <u>(easy to use)</u>

4. Laptop-To-Go is _____ Laptop-Friend.
   <u>(fast)</u>

5. The software package that comes with Laptop-To-Go is _____
   <u>(good)</u>
   the one that comes with Laptop-Friend.

6. Laptop-To-Go is _____ Laptop-Friend.
   <u>(heavy)</u>

6 WHAT ABOUT YOU? Which laptop computer would <u>you</u> buy? Explain your reasons, using **as . . . as** and some of the adverbs from Exercise 5.

LESSON 2

7 Match each action with the correct purpose. Write the letter on the line.

1. He enrolled in an electronics course because he ____.

2. She went to the electronics store because she ____.

3. I bought speakers because I ____.

4. He turned on the television because he ____.

5. She bought a palm pilot because she ____.

a. needed to buy a printer

b. needed to be more organized

c. wanted to learn how to repair computers

d. wanted to listen to music on the computer

e. wanted to watch the news

8 Rewrite the sentences in Exercise 7, using infinitives of purpose.

1. _He enrolled in an electronics course to learn how to repair computers_ .

2. _____ .

3. _____ .

4. _____ .

5. _____ .

9 Use the icon prompts to complete the conversation.

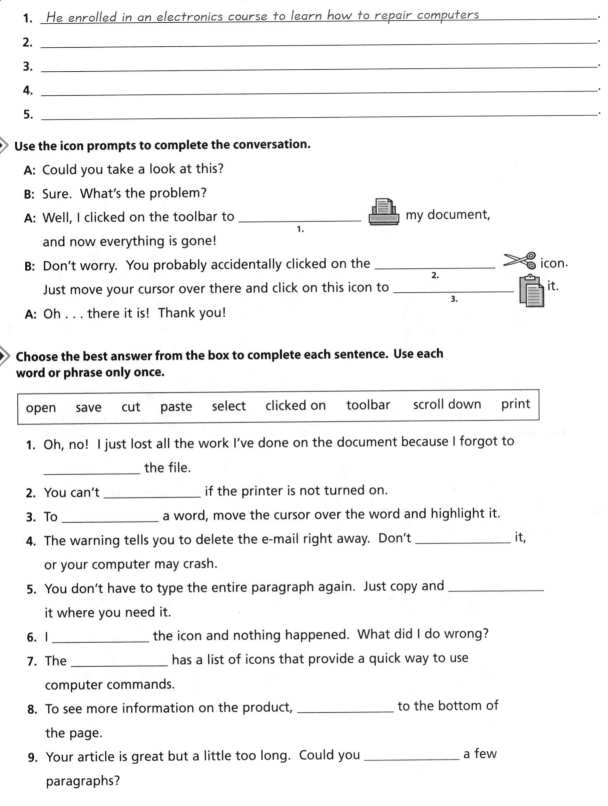

A: Could you take a look at this?

B: Sure. What's the problem?

A: Well, I clicked on the toolbar to _____ my document,
and now everything is gone!
     1.

B: Don't worry. You probably accidentally clicked on the _____ icon.
Just move your cursor over there and click on this icon to _____ it.
     2.
     3.

A: Oh . . . there it is! Thank you!

10 Choose the best answer from the box to complete each sentence. Use each
word or phrase only once.

open	save	cut	paste	select	clicked on	toolbar	scroll down	print

1. Oh, no! I just lost all the work I've done on the document because I forgot to
   _____ the file.

2. You can't _____ if the printer is not turned on.

3. To _____ a word, move the cursor over the word and highlight it.

4. The warning tells you to delete the e-mail right away. Don't _____ it,
   or your computer may crash.

5. You don't have to type the entire paragraph again. Just copy and _____
   it where you need it.

6. I _____ the icon and nothing happened. What did I do wrong?

7. The _____ has a list of icons that provide a quick way to use
   computer commands.

8. To see more information on the product, _____ to the bottom of
   the page.

9. Your article is great but a little too long. Could you _____ a few
   paragraphs?

LESSON 3

11 Here's how some people use their computers. Look at the pictures and complete the sentences, using infinitives of purpose.

1. Ivana uses her computer *to join a chat room*.

3. Edward uses his computer _____.

5. Liana uses her computer _____.

7. Abby uses the scanner _____ into the computer.

2. Theresa uses the computer _____.

4. Frank uses his computer _____.

6. Martin uses his computer _____.

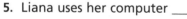

12 Read about how these people use the computer. Who is speaking? Choose one of the people from Exercise 11. Write the person's name under his or her picture.

I'm a fashion designer, and I really need to learn about what people wear and why they wear it. So I joined this chat room to talk with other people about fashion.

I have a lot of friends, and I like to keep in touch with them. So I send instant messages all the time.

I spend about eight hours a day surfing the Internet. I just love it. I guess you could say I'm a computer addict.

1. *Ivana*

2. _____

3. _____

I just graduated, so I created my own website to keep in touch with my classmates. It's been a lot of work. I used to surf the Internet all the time, but now I spend all my time creating and updating the website.

I'm a big music fan, so I've been using my computer to download music files. My friend just sent me a new song to download. Here . . . want to listen?

4. _____

5. _____

 13 WHAT ABOUT YOU? Write a paragraph about how **you** use the computer. Be sure to answer these questions in your paragraph.

- How many hours do you use the computer each week?
- Do you use the computer more for work or for fun?
- Would you rather spend more time with people or with the computer?

LESSON 4

14 Read the online advice column. Then answer the questions.

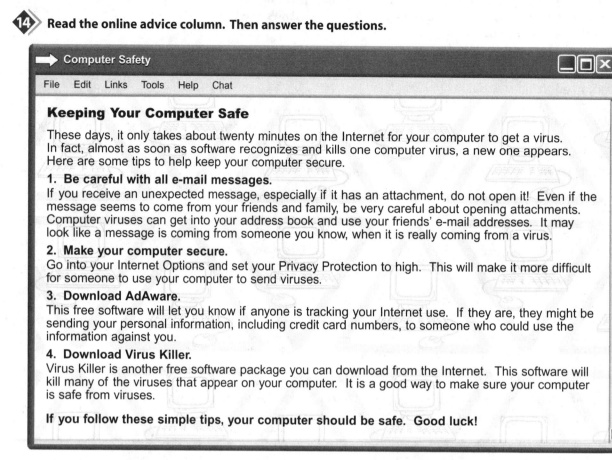

Computer Safety

File   Edit   Links   Tools   Help   Chat

Keeping Your Computer Safe

These days, it only takes about twenty minutes on the Internet for your computer to get a virus. In fact, almost as soon as software recognizes and kills one computer virus, a new one appears. Here are some tips to help keep your computer secure.

1. Be careful with all e-mail messages.
If you receive an unexpected message, especially if it has an attachment, do not open it! Even if the message seems to come from your friends and family, be very careful about opening attachments. Computer viruses can get into your address book and use your friends' e-mail addresses. It may look like a message is coming from someone you know, when it is really coming from a virus.

2. Make your computer secure.
Go into your Internet Options and set your Privacy Protection to high. This will make it more difficult for someone to use your computer to send viruses.

3. Download AdAware.
This free software will let you know if anyone is tracking your Internet use. If they are, they might be sending your personal information, including credit card numbers, to someone who could use the information against you.

4. Download Virus Killer.
Virus Killer is another free software package you can download from the Internet. This software will kill many of the viruses that appear on your computer. It is a good way to make sure your computer is safe from viruses.

If you follow these simple tips, your computer should be safe. Good luck!

SOURCE: www.ncl.ac.uk

1. What can you do to prevent someone from using your computer to send viruses?

_____.

2. Why does the article suggest downloading the two kinds of software?

_____.

3. How can a virus use the address book in your computer?

_____.

4. Why do you have to be careful about e-mails from people you know?

_____.

15 WHAT ABOUT YOU? Write a paragraph about what you have done, or what you would like to do, to keep your computer safe.

GRAMMAR
BOOSTER

A Look at the video game report cards. Write sentences comparing A–1 and Game Plan. Use the comparative form of the adjective or adverb in parentheses.

Video Game Reports	A–1	
	0 ← → 10	
Sound quality		(5)
Visual quality		(8)
Interest level		(4)
Fun level		(6)
Violence level		(8)
Easy to play		(4)
Speed		(7)
Price	$89.95	

Video Game Reports	Game Plan	
	0 ← → 10	
Sound quality		(4)
Visual quality		(5)
Interest level		(8)
Fun level		(6)
Violence level		(7)
Easy to play		(7)
Speed		(4)
Price	$129.95	

1. A–1 sounds _better than Game Plan_ .
   (good)

2. Game Plan is _____ .
   (interesting)

3. Game Plan is _____ .
   (violent)

4. Game Plan is _____ .
   (easy to play)

5. A–1 looks _____ .
   (good)

6. A–1 is _____ .
   (expensive)

7. A–1 runs _____ .
   (fast)

B Now look at the report card for a third video game. Write sentences comparing all three video games, using the superlative form of the adjective or adverb in parentheses.

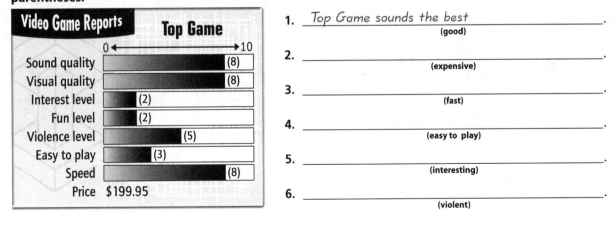

Video Game Reports	Top Game	
	0 ← → 10	
Sound quality		(8)
Visual quality		(8)
Interest level		(2)
Fun level		(2)
Violence level		(5)
Easy to play		(3)
Speed		(8)
Price	$199.95	

1. _Top Game sounds the best_ .
   (good)

2. _____ .
   (expensive)

3. _____ .
   (fast)

4. _____ .
   (easy to play)

5. _____ .
   (interesting)

6. _____ .
   (violent)

C ▷ Complete each sentence with the correct form of the adjective in parentheses.

1. I shop online for computer products. It's much _____ than going to a computer store. (easy)

2. Of all the printers in the store, the R100 is definitely the _____. (quiet)

3. This is the _____ movie I've ever seen. (romantic)

4. Jessica's oil paintings are gorgeous. Her pencil drawings are just as _____. (charming)

5. The Bax monitor is not big enough. I need something even _____. (big)

6. The traffic on my way to work was very slow. Luckily, the traffic on my way home was not nearly as _____. (bad)

7. We've never had a _____ vacation than this one. It was so much fun! (exciting)

D ▷ Read the conversation. Find all the infinitives that express a purpose. Underline the sentences.

A: It's 6:00. Are you going home?

B: No, I'm staying late to finish this report. How about you?

A: I'm leaving now. I'm going to stop at Big Box to buy a new scanner. Then I'm going to ComputerWorld to get something on sale.

B: Really? What?

A: I'm looking for a new laptop computer.

B: What's wrong with your home computer?

A: Nothing. But the kids use it to surf the Internet all the time.

B: What do they do online?

A: Oh, everything. They use the computer to get e-mail, to download music, to chat with their friends, and to order stuff from online stores.

E ▷ Rewrite the sentences you underlined in Exercise D. Use <u>in order to</u>.

1. *I'm staying late in order to finish this report* _____.
2. _____.
3. _____.
4. _____.
5. _____.

F ▷ CHALLENGE. Rewrite Speaker A's last sentence in Exercise D again, using <u>for</u> this time. (Remember to change the verbs into gerunds!)

_____

_____

Complete the sentences with <u>for</u> or <u>to</u>.

1. I like to shop online _____ delicious foods from Italy.

2. My son uses the computer _____ download music.

3. Judith e-mailed me _____ directions to the party.

4. Daniel uses the Internet _____ get the latest news.

5. Sheila e-mailed her mother _____ say she bought a new computer.

H **CHALLENGE. WHAT ABOUT YOU? Complete the sentences, using your <u>own</u> words. Use an infinitive of purpose or <u>for</u>.**

1. I log on to the Internet _____ .

2. I'd buy a new printer _____ .

3. I'd get a digital camera _____ .

JUST FOR **FUN**

1 **WORD FIND. Find the words listed below. The words are across (→), down (↓), diagonal (↘), and sometimes backwards (←). Circle the words. Then find the hidden message. (Hint: Read the letters <u>not</u> circled in the first four lines.)**

click on	N	W	O	D	L	L	U	P	S	E	T	R	C	U	O
crashed	C	L	I	C	K	O	N	U	E	S	B	L	R	N	E
cursor	S	C	R	O	L	L	S	H	L	U	O	R	A	E	O
cut	T	A	P	R	O	B	L	E	E	O	M	O	S	M	O
file	O	M	I	J	D	C	P	P	C	M	R	S	H	C	D
icon	Y	G	T	X	Q	L	Q	E	T	I	Z	R	E	U	K
menu	R	Y	F	E	U	F	G	R	F	D	Z	U	D	T	A
mouse	V	A	O	C	X	C	T	M	O	A	J	C	A	C	D
paste	Z	O	B	Q	H	J	N	F	I	L	E	D	E	J	M
print	I	A	V	L	T	R	I	S	E	E	T	S	A	P	M
pull down	K	C	B	W	O	L	R	P	O	L	W	C	B	J	D
scroll	G	Q	O	K	V	O	P	C	V	E	W	G	V	Z	D
select	P	J	W	N	H	Y	T	J	B	O	X	F	J	H	F
toolbar	F	C	G	A	A	F	M	T	S	O	I	Z	Y	K	Q
	R	C	J	J	P	G	N	H	Z	V	P	Z	R	W	O

Hidden message: _____

POPULAR SAYINGS. Here are the beginnings and endings of some traditional expressions using <u>as</u> . . . <u>as</u>. See how many you can put together correctly. After you finish, check your answers.

as	black cold flat good old pretty quiet white	as	gold a mouse the hills ice night a pancake a picture a sheet

as old as the hills

_____

_____

_____

_____

_____

_____

Which of these sayings are similar to ones you know in your native language?

_____

_____

_____

Which are different?

_____

_____

_____

_____

UNIT 10

Ethics and Values

TOPIC PREVIEW

1 Read the letters to the advice columnist. What advice do you think the columnist may give? Check the box.

→ Amanda's Advice ☐ ☐ ☒

◁ Back ▷ Forward ⟳ Reload ✕ Stop 🏠 Home 🔍 Search

Do you have any ethical questions? Write to Amanda.

① Dear Amanda:
I reserved a compact rental car, but when I went to pick it up, they gave me a luxury car for the same price. Should I tell them that they made a mistake?
Paul
Click Here for Amanda's Advice

② Dear Amanda:
My favorite shampoo had the wrong price on it. It was half the usual price, so I bought ten bottles. Do you think that's OK?
Helena
Click Here for Amanda's Advice

③ Dear Amanda:
I rented five DVDs this morning at my local video store. The clerk only charged me the rental fee for three. I didn't say anything. Should I tell the clerk when I return the DVDs?
Samantha
Click Here for Amanda's Advice

④ Dear Amanda:
Yesterday I saw someone get on my hotel's free airport shuttle bus. I know she wasn't staying at the hotel. Should I complain to the hotel manager?
George
Click Here for Amanda's Advice

---

1. ☐ Paul should tell the rental company they made a mistake and offer to pay for the luxury car.

   ☐ Paul should stop worrying and enjoy his luxury car.

2. ☐ Helena should feel great about saving money.

   ☐ Helena should go back and tell the store manager the price was wrong and pay the correct price.

3. ☐ Samantha should tell the clerk that she wasn't charged for 2 DVDs.

   ☐ Samantha should just relax and enjoy the DVDs without telling the clerk.

4. ☐ George should tell the hotel manager about the person using the shuttle bus.

   ☐ George should mind his own business and not complain about someone else.

2 WHAT ABOUT YOU? Have you ever had a similar experience to any of these situations? Write a paragraph about what you did.

3 Look at the pictures showing what some teenagers want to do. Do you think each person needs to ask for permission or not?

☐ needs permission
☐ doesn't need permission
☐ it depends (explain) _____

_____

☐ needs permission
☐ doesn't need permission
☐ it depends (explain) _____

_____

☐ needs permission
☐ doesn't need permission
☐ it depends (explain) _____

_____

☐ needs permission
☐ doesn't need permission
☐ it depends (explain) _____

_____

☐ needs permission
☐ doesn't need permission
☐ it depends (explain) _____

_____

LESSON 1

4 Circle the correct words to complete the conversations.

1. **A:** Where should we watch the game after work?

   B: Let's go to your house. (Your / Yours) TV is much bigger than (my / mine).

2. **A:** Is this (our / ours) room?

   B: No, we have a suite, and this is a single, so this is definitely not (our / ours).

3. **A:** Is this car key (your / yours)?

   B: No, it's not (my / mine). I don't even have a car!

4. **A:** Whose books are these? (Him / His) or (her / hers)?

   B: I don't know. Ask them if they're (their / theirs).

5. **A:** Who has traveled more? Your parents or (mine / my)?

   B: (Your / Yours) parents, I think. (My / Mine) parents don't travel much at all.

86 UNIT 10

5 Change each sentence into a sentence using a possessive pronoun.

1. The shaving cream is George's. _The shaving cream is his_____.

2. The hair spray is Judy's. _____.

3. The toothbrushes are Amy and Mark's. _____.

4. The razors are George's. _____.

5. The shampoo is everyone's. _____.

6 Look at the pictures and complete the conversations with possessive adjectives or possessive pronouns.

1. **A:** Excuse me. I think you forgot something.

   B: I did?

   A: Isn't that cell phone _____?

   B: No, it isn't. It must be _____.

2. **A:** Is this _____?

   B: No, it's not _____.

   It's _____ tip.

3. **A:** Is that book _____?

   B: No, it's _____ book.

4. **A:** Are these earrings _____?

   B: No, they're not _____.

   They're _____.

LESSON 2

7 Read the conversations. Summarize the advice with present factual conditional sentences.

1. **A:** I don't have antivirus software.

   B: You shouldn't surf the Internet.

   If you don't have antivirus software, you shouldn't surf the Internet   .

2. **A:** I want to e-mail some photos to my friends.

   B: You have to scan them first.

   _____ .

3. **A:** I want to make friends on the Internet.

   B: You can join a chat room.

   _____ .

4. **A:** My computer crashes all the time.

   B: You'd better find out what's wrong.

   _____ .

8 CHALLENGE. Match the two parts of each conditional sentence. Write the letter on the line.

1. If you speak Spanish, you ____.   a. don't use sunscreen

2. If you spoke Spanish, you ____.   b. could work in South America

3. Your hair will look great if you ____. c. use this shampoo every day

4. If you took a taxi, you ____.   d. can travel all over Central America

5. You'll get sunburned if you ____.   e. would get to work faster

9 Rewrite the factual conditional sentences in the unreal conditional. Use the true statements in parentheses to help you.

1. If we go to Russia, I'll learn Russian. (We're not going to Russia.)

   If we went to Russia, I would learn Russian   .

2. If she has time, she'll read more. (She doesn't have time.)

   _____ .

3. If I need to lose weight, I'll avoid fatty foods. (I don't need to lose weight.)

   _____ .

10 Look at the pictures. Use the words and phrases in the box to complete the conversations.

| too much change   undercharged   didn't charge |

1. **A:** Look at this bill.

   B: What's wrong with it?

   A: They _____ us. Look.

   They _____ us for the drinks

   or for the desserts.

   B: I guess we'd better tell them.

2. **A:** What's wrong?

   B: I think the clerk gave me _____.
   I should have only two euros back in change, but
   she gave me twelve!

   A: I'll try to get her attention . . . Excuse me?

LESSON 3

 11 **Read about these people's personal values. How would you describe
each person? Write the name on the line.**

James

I love tattoos. But they
should be for men only.
Women should always have
clear, beautiful skin. And they
should just stay at home and
look after the children.

Dina

I'm not comfortable wearing
clothes that show too much
of my body.

Tessa

I think it's fine for young men
and women to get their
bodies pierced if they want to.
But if you're over forty, you
really shouldn't. It just looks
silly!

Hazel

People used to dress
formally when they went to
the opera. Now some
people wear jeans to the
opera. It's just not
appropriate!

1. Who is old-fashioned? _____

2. Who is sexist? _____

3. Who thinks modesty is important? _____

4. Who has a double standard? _____

12 **WHAT ABOUT YOU? Whose personal values are closest to yours? Complete the
paragraph. Explain your opinions and give examples.**

My personal values are closest to _____'s values.

LESSON 4

13 Read the home page of the Internet Lost-and-Found. Then choose the best answers to the questions below. Circle the letter.

→ Internet Lost-and-Found   ⬁ ☐ ☒

Welcome to the Internet Lost-and-Found.

The Internet Lost-and-Found

REPORT   RETURN   REWARD

If you've lost something, here's where you'll find it!

It's simple to use our website.
If you've lost something, enter your lost item into our database. <u>Click here</u>.
If you've found something, enter the found item into our database. <u>Click here</u>.

Search our easy-to-use database.

Search hotel lost-and-founds. Enter the city code here.

Search airport lost-and-founds. Enter the airport code here.

Search bus and subway lost-and-founds. Enter the city code here.

Internet Lost-and-Found Statistics Worldwide

Lost Items: 48,806
Found Items: 19,819

Lost-and-Found Story of the Week

We were on vacation when my daughter lost her gold ring. She looked everywhere but could not find it. She was very sad about it. Then she went to <u>lostandfound.com</u> and entered it into the database. One day later, someone called. A hotel guest found it in the hotel fitness center. My daughter was so excited. If we had waited one more day, we would have gone back home and never seen the ring again. We never met the hotel guest who returned the ring. But we want to say thank you so much!

The Jones Family

---

1. What did the Jones family lose?

   a. their daughter   b. their daughter's ring   c. their vacation

2. Where were they when they lost it?

   a. on vacation   b. at work   c. in the car

3. Where did someone find it?

   a. at the airport   b. in the bathroom   c. in the fitness center

4. If you lose something at an airport and want to find it on the Internet Lost-and-Found, what should you do?

   a. enter the city code   b. enter the airport code   c. enter the airport name

14 WHAT ABOUT YOU? What would <u>you</u> do if you found a gold ring in a hotel fitness center?

GRAMMAR BOOSTER

A CHALLENGE. **Read the statements and then complete the factual conditional sentences.**

1. I usually go jogging every day, unless it rains.

   If it doesn't rain, _I go jogging_____ .

2. I like driving short distances, but for longer distances, I always fly.

   _____ if I have to travel longer distances.

3. I never drink coffee after dinner. I can't fall asleep at night when I do.

   _____, I can't fall asleep at night.

4. It rarely snows here. The schools close whenever more than a centimeter falls.

   _____ if it snows more than a centimeter.

5. I never watch horror movies before bed. I just can't get to sleep!

   _____, I can't get to sleep.

B **Rewrite the factual conditional sentences in Exercise A, reversing the clauses and using commas where necessary.**

1. _I go jogging if it doesn't rain_____ .

2. _____ .

3. _____ .

4. _____ .

5. _____ .

C **Choose the correct form to complete each present or future factual conditional sentence.**

1. If they _____ the musical, they _____ it again tomorrow.

   like / will like   **see / will see**

2. If Fernando _____ comedies, he _____ a lot.

   watched / watches   **laughed / laughs**

3. If you _____ some ice cream, I _____ you eat it.

   buy / will buy   **help / will help**

4. If I _____ fall asleep, I usually _____ a lot of work done

   won't / don't   **get / got**

   in the evening.

5. _____ to England if your boss _____ you there next month?

   Will you travel / Do you travel   **needs / will need**

6. Always _____ your seat belt if you _____ to be safe.

   wear / wore   **want / will want**

7. I _____ a tattoo if my parents _____ me not to.

   didn't got / won't get   **tell / told**

8. If I _____ my mother for permission, she _____ no.

   ask / will ask   **say / will say**

9. If I _____ far, I always _____ .

   travel / will travel   **fly / flew**

D Use the moral dilemmas to ask and answer questions, using the unreal conditional.

1. **Moral dilemma:** You found someone's credit card in a restaurant.

   Q: _What would you do if_ _____ ?

   A: _If I_ _____ .

2. **Moral dilemma:** The drugstore didn't charge you for some items.

   Q: _____ ?

   A: _____ .

JUST FOR
FUN

1 Complete the sentences. Then put the numbered letters in order. You will write an English proverb.

1. Those shoes are my shoes. Those shoes are ___ ___ ___ .

                                                                        1   2

2. When there are different rules for different people, it is a

   ___ ___ ___ ___ ___ ___ ___ ___ ___ ___ ___ ___ ___ .

                  3   4

3. Lipstick, eye shadow, and mascara are all ___ ___ ___ ___ ___ ___ ___ .

                                                                               5   6

4. Another way to say "you're welcome" is "___ ___ ___ ___ ___ ___ ___ ___ ___ ."

                                                     7   8   9

5. Another way to say "absolutely" is "___ ___ ___ ___ ___ ___ ___ ___ ."

                                  10   11

6. When someone has ideas from the past, we say he or she is

   ___ ___ ___ - ___ ___ ___ ___ ___ ___ ___ ___ .

                                         12

   Proverb: " ___ ___ ___ ___ ___ ___ ___ ___ ___ ___ ___ ___ ___ ___ ___ ___ ___ ___ ___ ___ ___ ___ ___ ."

             12 10   2   5   9   4   7   1   9   4 12   5   3   5   9   4   6 10   8   1 11   7

2 Think of five different ways to reply to "Thank you." Write them on the lines below.

1. ___ Y ___ L ___ (___) ___ ___ E

2. ___ ___ N' ___ ___ ___ N (___) ___ ___ ___ I (___)

3. N ___ (___) A ___ ___ L ___

4. ___ O ___ R (___) ___ E ___

5. ___ (___) ___ ' ___ E ___ ___ L ___ O ___ ___

Now unscramble the circled letters above to make a word.

This is something teenagers should get permission for. ___ ___ ___ ___ ___ ___